PARENT, CHILD, AND ADOLESCENT

Understanding and Care

PARENT, CHILD, AND ADOLESCENT

Understanding and Care

Victor M. Uribe, M.D.

About The Book

Here is a handbook that gives the reasons for and the answers to the problems that confront parents, children, and adolescents.

Dr. Victor Uribe, a noted adult, adolescent, and child psychiatrist, draws on his many years of experience to clearly and non-judgmentally examine family interactions and offer solutions to problems that face all families. Some of the topics covered include:

- Why children behave as they do
- Why adolescents behave as they do
- Sexuality
- Attention Deficit Hyperactive Disorder
- Disorders of eating habits and nutrition
- Normal and abnormal anxiety
- Panic disorder
- Self-abusive drug misuse
- Lists of addictive drugs, their street names, and effects
- Self-abusive alcohol misuse
- Mood disorders in children and adolescents
- Choosing a therapist
- And much, much more!

Acknowledgments

I thank Martha, Sonia, and Liliana Uribe; David Scherer; Michael J. McGowan; Eduardo Machado; and Glen Wurglitz, for their helpful comments; and Marguerite Henderson for her extensive and useful comments and for retyping the revised versions of the manuscript.

Dedication

With special love, I dedicate this book to my parents, brothers and sisters, and as well as to Martha, Sonia, Bryan Andres, Michael Javier, Bryanna Beatriz, Stephanie Cristina, Matthew Victor Richard, and Kyle Victor, my family.

x

Contents

Authors Note

This book is designed to provide you with accurate information and guidance about behavioral problems of children and adolescents and about parent, child, and adolescent interpersonal relationships. However, your situation may be different from the ones presented in this book. Information of this type will not provide the same results for everyone. As a result, this book is written and sold with the understanding that neither the author nor the publisher is engaged in rendering specific medical and psychiatric services to any individual. Consult your own physician or psychiatric consultant for further information about conditions and other issues discussed in this book. The case illustrations are clinically valid mixtures of evaluation, diagnosis, therapy, and follow-up results, but they do not specify individual patients. Names of patients and other identification data are fictitious.

Preface

Parent, Child, and Adolescent: Understanding and Care is a straight forward presentation of childhood and the complexities related to child development. It outlines some of the general concepts of what parents can expect, as well as those few things that can crop up and are particularly vexing for parents.

The book is presented in a "plain English" format that will be easy for most parents to understand. Designed for parents and other lay people, in a most unpretentious fashion, this book provides a bit of information, a bit of guidance, and a lot of hope for folks who pay serious attention to the responsibilities and demands of parenting.

For parents, grandparents, teachers, and lay people who are interested in children and child rearing, this book will be pleasant and easy reading and an important stimulus for further thinking and study about children and the vicissitude of child rearing.

Bennett L. Leventhal, M.D.
Professor of Psychiatry and Pediatrics
Director, Child and Adolescent Psychiatry
Chairman (Interim), Department of Psychiatry
The University of Chicago

Foreword

Parents wish to perform as well as they can on behalf of their children. But families across America are beset with concerns regarding violence, drugs, mental illness, teenage pregnancies, learning problems, and school dropouts.

This book explains the vectors and influences that shape our children's lives. It provides explanations and approaches to raising emotionally healthy children. Yet, not all children will grow without emotional or stressful impositions on their development. Their families can benefit from the knowledge in dealing with the problems that may arise as the child grows through the successive stages of development.

Each threshold holds both promises and dangers for the outcomes into adulthood. While they root some problems that appear in a genetic predisposition to illness, others derive from chemical imbalances, environmental stresses, or the exaggerated anxieties imposed by peers or relationships.

An intelligent understanding of the normal processes of development can help us to bolster the child's self-esteem and increase the potentials inherent in all of our children. When an illness or disorder arises, knowing about the mechanisms which drive the symptoms can aid in the recovery.

Every parent has the capacity to be a healer in concert with the professionals dealing with disorders.

This book leads the parent, the relative, the friend, through a well-written approach to understanding the healthy as well as the disturbed aspects of childhood and adolescence.

Harold M. Visotsky, M.D.
Owen L. Coon Professor
Psychiatry and Behavior Sciences
Northwestern University Medical School

CHAPTER 1

Introduction

Today a promise of "satisfaction guaranteed or your money back" protects consumers against most defective products. Coffee maker won't perk? Send it back. Vacuum doesn't work? Trade it in for a new model. But no such warranty or trade-in policy accompanies a far more fragile and precious commodity, your child.

Many parents who have high expectations about their adorable and even-tempered infant are often bewildered when the same child evolves as a "cranky or restless" baby, a "combative or hyperactive" child or as a "sullen, out-of-control" teenager.

No special skills or strategies are needed to raise a placid and affectionate child. It's those children and teens with difficult problems and often unmanageable behavior that challenge parents who are unprepared to cope, especially when they are already beset with other problems.

The disorders included in this book vary widely in terms of causes, severity, management and treatment. For example, a child's anxiety over a parent's job loss or pending divorce is perhaps less complic0ted to evaluate and treat than the uphill struggle of parents coping with an adolescent with a serious drug disorder and its related problems.

The first disorder can be treated by listening, reassurance, and massive doses of Tender Loving Care, while the other usually requires an unyielding and exhaustive-to-enforce policy of Tough Love and professional help.

But, whatever the disorder, the first step parents must take is to recognize the problem(s) and to assume responsibility of helping their youngsters to heal.

Ten year old Ron's parents both work and are struggling to keep afloat with their seven children. He is especially vulnerable because his parents don't believe in talking about feelings or telling their children they love them. Ron fights at school, has no friends, and has been caught smoking, drinking, and torturing animals.

Unless someone intervenes to buoy Ron's self confidence, nurture his sense of self-worth by telling him that he is really "somebody," and help him resolve his problems, his present behavior will only become worse.

Unlike Ron's parents who are apparently unwilling to change, you must become proactive in your child's behalf and decide to eliminate whatever it is in your life and in his or her environment that is having a negative impact on your youngster. This is not always easy and requires a high degree of determination and perseverance. But nothing will change unless you consciously want to change it and help your youngster to do likewise.

You may start by being open to the possibility that history may be repeating itself if you recognize some of your own shortcomings in your child or teenager. "I was just as stubborn and strong-willed as she is and smoke, drank and used drugs when I was her age," said one exasperated mother about her 13 year old daughter who has recently begun to experiment with alcohol and other addictive drugs.

The good news is that, strange as it may seem, conflicts between child and parents can actually be viewed positively. If you don't care about your youngster who is driving you crazy, why would you bother to try and change his or her behavior?

The bad news is that many parents don't know how to constructively change their child or adolescent's behavior. An important first step is to open the lines of communication.

For example, if you are distressed by your seven year old who is smoking or by your adolescent who is sexually promiscuous, let them know exactly how you feel. At the same time without humiliating, denigrating, or abusing them, give them the opportunity to express their own feelings about their behavior. Listen with empathy.

However, you don't have to grit your teeth and accept their actions just to keep the peace. In fact, you can do a lot to clear the air by simply saying: "Because I love you, I can't accept the fact that you're smoking or sleeping around. If you continue to do these things you're going to be badly hurt and you will have to face the negative consequences. I care about you and want to help you, and, if necessary, we'll seek professional help."

Then, listen carefully to your son or daughter if they decide to open their hearts and share their feelings and opinions and even their criticisms about you.

If nothing is ever done, nothing will ever change. You have to be willing to confront the issue. But when you do, be prepared to give valid reasons and then follow through and make the necessary changes.

Today, many school districts across the country are debating the need to introduce instruction on "values" into their curriculum. While viewed as essential by many educators, it is also a controversial commentary on our society that it is necessary to teach children in the classroom basic values that, for generations, were caught, rather than taught in the home.

Let me explain. Children imitate and identify with adults who are important to them such as parents, siblings, grandparents, aunts, uncles, and other family members. In the process they internalize these adults' values, making them their own.

But children are also not robots and can reject some or most of the values prized by their families, learning instead another set of ideals.

Not too long ago most people believed that -- for better or worse -- a child's home environment was the primary influence on his or her behavior. But the world has turned a few times and now we're more aware of outside forces that take precedent in shaping a child's values today.

These influences include peer pressure, counterculture values about sexuality and the family portrayed by some in the mass media, the easy availability of alcohol and other addicting drugs, and even the often unsettling political and economic climate, which all act as powerful magnets continually pulling youngsters away from the values they have been taught in their homes.

Let's face it. Raising a child today can be especially challenging to parents. If some encounters with your adolescent are distressing, don't despair. You're not alone. Few parents have come through these mutinous years unscathed.

It is difficult for parents to feel at ease all the time when faced with an unruly child or teen who is outspoken and continually questioning and defying your authority and values. But when you examine your youngster's behavior in context with many popular trends in society and the signals he or she is picking up from some segments of the media and even from adults outside your family, maybe his or her behavior isn't so outrageous or even so inappropriate after all.

Examples abound, such as the child whose response to your request to follow some basic rules is a defiant: "You can't tell me what to do!" Or the teen who sees nothing wrong with sleeping around because "everyone's doing it."

Like it or not, from the teens perspective of what they are bombarded with in some of today's most popular sitcoms as well as what is happening in some segments of society in general, they are absolutely right.

Values and life-styles that the vast majority of Americans consider unacceptable are portrayed as the "norm" in many of today's most popular programs marketed to adolescents. These programs present a slick and distorted picture of life in which characters use sarcasm and flippant put downs to neatly resolve ambiguous situations and thorny moral problems -- all before the final commercial! Hardly a reflection of the real world where consequences -- both good and bad -- follow our actions.

The powerful messages young people are receiving of "say no to guilt" and "if it's fun go for it now before it's too late" are much more attractive than the messages of personal responsibility and restraint they are hearing at home.

Today most parents still are in control of the ground rules at home. However, it's apparent that the battle to control the rules outside the home has been won by some powerful arbiters of popular culture.

This is a loss not only for parents but for American society as a whole. To regain these lost values requires the combined actions of parents, print and electronic media, government officials, and religious and other secular leaders.

For you as parents, there are no easy solutions on how to deal with your youngster's behavioral problems. However, the following guidelines, if used consistently, should help resolve or at least decrease the conflict between you and your son or daughter in the management of his or her behavioral problems:

1. Consider your youngster's talents and abilities and do not expect your child to do something that is not "do-able" for him or her. For example, the teen who turns to drugs and appears rudderless may be reacting to pressure from parents to go to college when, in fact, he has no interest in academics but would do well pursuing a trade.

2. Identify only the behavior as unacceptable and not your son or daughter, when your teen comes home well past curfew say "I was worried that something had happened to you" rather than, "What else can I expect from an undependable jerk like you."

3. Never attack your child's fragile sense of worth or self-esteem. Words can hurt and the damage inflicted on a youngster by a parent's thoughtless remarks can traumatize him or her for life. Some youngsters are able to shrug off put- downs, but others believe that if their parents say they're dumb, no good, and a failure, then it must be true.

4. Lay the ground rules of what is and is not acceptable behavior, and then be prepared to enforce them. A kid whose outside world may be in continual turmoil needs to know what to expect at home. Be consistent in setting limits and in your punishment, but still be available to listen with empathy and, when appropriate, be willing to modify your reaction.

5. If you feel you are in danger of losing your self-control because of your child's or teen's words or actions, remove yourself from the scene. Leave the room. Take a

walk. Call a friend. Have no further contact with your youngster until you've calmed down.
6. Recognize that the objectionable behavior may be only temporary. Nothing lasts forever. And if you can hang in there your terrible two year old will eventually turn three.
7. Be aware of the developmental stages your child goes through. Don't expect more of your youngster than is developmentally possible. Children grow in spurts and starts. Their development is spotty and performance that is low in one area today may excel next year.
8. Look for sources of support within and outside of your family. It will help you realize that you are not alone and your problems are not unique. Before seeking professional help try to find a support group in your community. You may also find it's often helpful to talk with good and trusted friends who have been through the same thing themselves.

In this book I outline strategies that parents can use, in addition to the guidelines, to help their children and teens who are struggling with afflictions including attention deficit hyperactivity, eating, anxiety, panic, phobic, posttraumatic, sexual, mood, and other disorders as well as self-abusive behavior involving alcohol and other addictive drugs. I also discuss devices youngsters can use to help themselves to cope with such disorders.

This book also includes chapters on professional consultations, dynamic medical psychotherapy, adolescents and world peace, and why children and adolescents behave the way they do.

During the past twenty five years, I have tested the guidelines discussed above and the self-help strategies outlined throughout this book, and I have observed that their consistent use can eliminate, or at least decrease some of the problems related to the disorders discussed in the following chapters.

CHAPTER 2

Attention Deficit Hyperactivity Disorder

When nine-year-old Tommy's parents brought him to my office for a consultation, it was apparent they were at the end of their rope. After three suspensions in the last nine months for disruptive behavior, Tommy had just been expelled from school.

Tommy's teachers had no trouble providing his parents with a long list of his faults including nonstop talking, interrupting others, hitting classmates and generally being unmanageable. But, they were short on solutions for his behavioral problems, suggesting only that the third grader should be hospitalized or sent to a residential school --anywhere, it seemed, as long as it was not their school.

And, realistically, who could blame them? According to his homeroom teacher, Tommy didn't follow directions, rarely finished his work when he even bothered to do it, or worse, didn't seem to care. "He does things in a hurry. He can't sit still, doesn't concentrate and won't wait for his turn. He throws pencils, erasers and anything else he can get his hands on," she added.

"We've tried everything from grounding him when he misbehaves to rewarding him when there seems to be an improvement, but nothing works. Now the school has given up on him. If they can't handle him what are we supposed to do?" Tommy's father complained.

What indeed! At the center of this war of words sat Tommy, fidgeting and twisting the buttons on his shirt. When I asked him what was troubling him, Tommy became defensive. "I don't know what's wrong with me," he said, agitatedly. "The kids all hate me. They don't want to play with me. They make fun of me and call me stupid, weird, retarded, crazy. Maybe I am crazy."

But after evaluating his personal, family and school history and examining him, I was able to reassure Tommy and his parents that he was none of these things. Tommy suffered not from a specific illness, but rather from a cluster of symptoms that have been labeled "Attention Deficit Hyperactivity

Disorder" (ADHD). These symptoms fall into one of three distinct groups: *distractibility, impulsivity,* and *hyperactivity.*

Typically, *distractibility* is present in children who lose things, daydream, are forgetful and don't finish assigned tasks. *Irnpulsivity* is characterized by their not thinking before they speak or act, not waiting their turn, blurting out opinions and interrupting others. *Hyperactivity* describes those who are fidgety, and find it hard to sit still, and are frequently too active.

A child who exhibits just one of these symptoms can cause turmoil both at home and in the classroom. But, when a child displays symptoms from all three groups, the impact can be even more explosive -- as seen by the reaction to Tommy's behavior by those around him and his own feelings about himself.

If your child is going through a phase in which he or she shows hyperactivity, fights with other children and can't seem to concentrate in school, it does not necessarily mean that he or she is a victim of ADHD. Every child displays some of these traits at one time or another.

When should you be concerned? When these traits have been present since early childhood and are habitual. So, if your six-year-old suddenly shows disruptive behavior, and it happens only once or twice, then it is likely he or she does not have ADHD, but may have other problems.

But if, like Tommy, your child has shown distractibility, impulsivity and hyperactivity since infancy, he or she may indeed suffer from ADHD. For example, as a baby everything bothered Tommy. He was easily irritated by lights and noise, cried constantly, and continually moved around in his crib. This behavior became even more pronounced as he grew older.

Your child might have ADHD if his or her problems are as pervasive as Tommy's. Does your son or daughter exhibit the symptoms of ADHD at home, but is generally well-behaved in school and with friends? Or, like Tommy, are these symptoms baggage carried everywhere, causing havoc wherever he or she goes?

How widespread is ADHD and what children are most likely to be affected? It is estimated that ADHD is present in five to ten percent of all elementary school age children in the U.S. and that in about fifty percent of these children, the affliction may continue into adolescence, and for another fifteen to twenty percent into adulthood. ADHD is also more common in boys, with a ratio of five to ten boys diagnosed with the disorder to one girl.

What causes ADHD? No one knows. However, most researchers believe it is triggered by at least one or a combination of genetic, physical, social, and environmental problems. Studies show the following possible contributing factors: history of ADHD in family members; brain dysfunction or damage due to trauma, lead, alcohol, drugs, or other toxins; malnutrition; vitamin deficiency; and reaction to food additives. Conventional neurological and other medical evaluations do not demonstrate evidence of gross structural damage or disease in the central nervous system. In addition, most youngsters with brain injuries and other neurological disorders do not show hyperactivity.

Other suspected culprits include learning disabilities; a chaotic family life; or a violent event or other problem that might frustrate a child's basic need for a calm, healthy, nurturing environment. Current research speculates that a deficiency of neurological transmitters in the brain may head the list as one of the leading causes of ADHD. So far, there is no conclusive evidence of neurophysiological or neuro-chemical cause. However, some children with this disorder may have minimal and subtle brain damage caused by diverse prenatal, perinatal, and postnatal problems. Such brain disorder may be related to the learning problems associated with ADHD.

Current treatment for Attention Deficit Hyperactivity Disorder consists of four therapies that include diet, counseling, behavior management, and medication. Some children improve with only one therapy, others respond with a combination, and still others experience a frustrating period of trial and error before the therapy most helpful for them can be pinpointed.

Diet is probably the least effective of the therapies. For years scientists have tried to link eating sugar, milk products, food coloring, seafood, and chocolate with hyperactivity, but as yet, there is no real scientific data to prove such a relationship.

Fortunately, counseling has proven to be an effective therapy in breaking the vicious cycle of the parents' distressing reactions to their child's unacceptable disruptive behavior and the child's resulting frustration, anxiety, depression, aggression, learning and at times socially unacceptable problems.

Medication has also proven to be extremely beneficial for many children between the ages of six and twelve. Paradoxically, the drugs that are most effective in controlling the hyperactivity and impulsive behavior of ADHD are stimulants such as dextroamphetamine, methylphenidate and pemoline. Stimulants do not "cure" but control the distressing symptoms in many children.

For reasons not yet understood these drugs improve a child's concentration, reaction time, and verbal and motor activity. However, they also can cause side effects, such as dizziness, headaches, dry mouth, nausea, insomnia, decreased appetite, abdominal pains, liver disturbances, lethargy. Other adverse effects are tremors, blood pressure changes, palpitations, cardiac dysrhythmias. Therefore, stimulant medications should only be prescribed when absolutely necessary, and need careful monitoring by a physician. Rarely are they prescribed for more than three years.

Parents who view medication and counseling as a last resort and who are able to look at their child's behavior objectively may be more comfortable -- and successful--following another approach, one of behavior management.

Behavior Management

- Accepting the child's problems
- Establishing a routine for play, study and chores--and sticking to it
- Eliminating negative stimulation such as monsters and violence on television, movies, Internet, and publications, and overly loud music from "boom boxes" and headset radios
- Providing a structured family environment with fair, flexible, but firm limits and controls
- Avoiding bribes and other manipulative coercion, and physical punishment
- Enforcing socially acceptable rules
- Rewarding appropriate behavior and correcting inappropriate behavior by restricting privileges accordingly
- Expressing consistent, but flexible attitudes and expectations
- Eliminating excessive permissiveness and excuses for misbehavior
- Emphasizing personal responsibility
- Giving brief and specific directions
- Showing consistency, patience, and a matter-of-fact communications and reaction

In Tommy's case, it was decided that drastic measures such as sending him to a facility away from home would do more harm than good. Instead, his parents opted for a recommended combination of medication, short term counseling, and a fresh approach to managing his behavior based on the strategies outlined above.

Prior to therapy, Tommy refused to do his chores or did them partially; watched movies of monsters, killers, robbers, and other violent scenes on the TV and used the Internet until about midnight; listened to one of his two "boomboxes" or to one of his three headset radios while going through the motions of doing his school assignments; hit his siblings, interrupted, and rarely listened to his parents and teachers.

Prior to therapy, the attitudes and reactions of Tommy's parents to his deviant behaviors shifted frequently and drastically -- from ignoring through permitting or even offering unstructured or irresponsible activities to bribing him with expensive and noisy toys, grounding him for two or three weeks, lecturing him, or calling him stupid, retarded, weird, and crazy.

By the end of therapy, Tommy was taking medication; he and his parents participated in counselling; and his parents established a flexible, firm and a matter-of-fact daily routine.

On arrival from school, he ate a snack while conversing with his mother about what he did with his teachers and peers; then, he watched 30 minutes of funny, nonviolent cartoons on TV; completed his teacher's assignments; then, he ate dinner with his parents and his siblings, waited for his turn to speak up, and did not listen to any of his noisy boomboxes or headset radios.

After dinner, under his parents' supervision, he played with programs for children on the Internet or watched children's shows on TV for one and a half hours; he then played ball or table games with his parents or siblings; read stories with any or all of them; and took a shower and put on his pajamas. He was in bed by eight thirty.

At the end of treatment, Tommy and his parents showed some of their former negative attitudes and reactions, but with less frequency, less intensity, less hostility, and less revenge.

This comprehensive approach helped Tommy and his parents. His parents began to enforce a consistent approach to discipline, and, equally important, learned to curb their impatience and anger. At the same time, they showed him love and support and with mutual collaboration with his teachers provided pertinent management and reactions that he needed in order to cope better with his problems.

In turn, Tommy began to learn what to expect both when he behaved appropriately, and when he broke the rules. He began to respond positively to the more relaxed attitude of his parents and teachers and to come to terms with his shortcomings. He also came to the realization that no one was "out to get him" and so eventually dropped the chip on his shoulder. He even began to like himself. As time went on, he still had occasional flare-ups, but they became the exception rather than daily occurrences.

What was important was obtaining professional help and a determination to change. What had become an intolerable situation became progressively rewarding for all concerned. Tommy and his parents took the important first steps toward healing. They worked together. They brought about changes that helped Tommy become proud of himself and more confident about what he could accomplish.

CHAPTER 3

Disorders of Eating Habits and Nutrition

"I cannot concentrate on anything... I do not go out with my friends as much . . . I can't study as I should . . · I'm afraid I will flunk... I cry almost everyday...I feel irritable, tired, weak.., doctors found nothing wrong with me . . · I don't know what to do . . . I feel terrible" said Caroline, during her initial visit.

After a prolonged hesitation, she cried "I don't know what is wrong with me. I have been doing something terrible. I have not told anybody about it, not even three doctors I saw recently, but now, I just cannot keep it a secret any longer. You see I have an urge to stuff myself and to vomit by putting my fingers in my throat. I cannot control it. I cannot stop it, I feel so awful, evil, ashamed of myself."

After a less hesitant and brief pause, Caroline said "I am thinking about my fear of gaining weight almost all the time. The doctors told me that I actually am underweight, that there is no reason for me to worry about gaining weight, that they found nothing to worry about, but I feel fat."

Caroline had seen a gynecologist due to "irregular menses," two internists due to "feeling weak and tired," and a cardiologist due to "palpitations and irregular cardiac rhythm at times." According to the physicians, there was not a demonstrable organic cause of her symptoms. They said that these were probably caused by the stress of college and her intense wish to excel in her studies.

Her overconcern with her body shape and weight began eighteen months before, when she turned seventeen and moved away from her family and friends to start college. "Since I began college I have felt that I would not be popular with guys, especially with the good looking ones, unless I was slim, and I felt that if I gained weight I would not be able to compete with so many thin and sexy girls at my school." said Caroline.

She explained, "At first I ate little for three or four days a week and I jogged and lifted weights three times a week, but it all got out of control. Lately, I ate very little three days a week, fasted one day, then ate a lot and vomited by putting my fingers down my throat. I have tried to stop doing it, but I cannot."

"A few weeks ago I got scared," said Caroline. She had read about the dental caries and loss of tooth enamel, and menstrual, muscular, gastrointestinal, cardiac and other serious health disorders caused by eating disorders. "I felt frightened when I read that such problems can become fatal." said Caroline.

Caroline had *bulimia nervosa.* Her symptoms were precipitated by her fear of moving away from her family and friends to live at college, by her competition with classmates, by her ambivalent dependency and independence, and by the increased educational, athletic, social, heterosexual and other pressures of college life.

In describing herself, she said "I am perfectionistic, ambitious, achievement-oriented. I want to be independent, but it seems hard." Her past history revealed mixed feelings and unresolved anger towards her neglectful mother; manipulative control of her eating since early childhood; intense critical evaluation of herself and others combined with a controlling, rigid and demanding attitude; and frequent frustration and deception about herself and others when things don't go the way she wanted them to.

Eating disorders are characterized by a deliberate decreased or increased intake of food resulting in loss or gain of weight, respectively, that may become life threatening.

Because of trendy publications, movies, and television programs, *anorexia nervosa, bulimia* and *obesity* are the most well-recognized of the eating disorders. However, there are others such as *rumination* and *pica* which can be just as disastrous to a youngster's health.

What causes eating disorders in children and adolescents? Often parents and caretakers themselves have eating problems and/or will not allow for differences in children's appetite and food preferences. The overweight grandmother pushing food toward her grandchildren, saying "Eat, eat, you are too thin," has become a caricature for comedians. But if food is overemphasized, either by forcing or exaggeratedly restricting the types and amounts of food to be eaten a youngster may develop aberrant eating behaviors.

Such disorders can also result from individual and social fads transmitted to children and adolescents. For instance, the child or adolescent who constantly witnesses his or her underweight mother obsessing with being fat and using self-imposed drastic diets and exaggerated exercising to lose weight, clearly gets an unhealthy message.

This is not to say that parents should not emphasize healthy eating habits, but *forcing* children to eat with rigid rules or pressing them directly or subtly to obsess about thinness can lead to conflictual interactions that contribute to eating and nutritional problems of a youngster. However, these disorders may result from additional causes, as in the eating disorders discussed below.

Rumination

Rumination is a rare disorder that occurs mostly between three and twelve months of age and is characterized by repeated re-chewing and re-swallowing or expelling of food, and failure to thrive. In extreme cases, it can cause death.

Rumination may appear in some infants whose parents or others restrain their arms, trying to stop their thumb sucking. The children then suck and chew on their tongue, causing food in their stomach to return to their mouth. As soon as this problem becomes apparent, and to prevent ruminating from becoming a habit, doctors advise parents to allow the child to suck his or her thumb, and to give solid and easily digestible meals, such as puddings or cereals, to their baby. It is also advisable to provide company and affectionate care to the infant.

Parents whose baby has this affliction need to consult a pediatrician and a child psychiatrist to evaluate the infant's physical status, the feeding process, and the relationship between the mother (or caretaker) and child to determine any physical and interpersonal problems. This type of evaluation is essential because rumination can be associated with specific physical ailments, such as disturbed motility or hernia of the esophagus, which require medical or surgical treatment. Rumination can also be a sign of impaired pa-rental-infant relationship or mental retardation, which requires specialized care.

Pica

Another eating disorder is called pica. It is characterized by a repetitive intake of non-nutritive substances. Pica has been reported in children, adolescents, and adults -- it is especially prevalent in poor and uneducated pregnant women who cannot afford nutritional foods.

In other cases, infants may eat paint, plaster, string, hair or cloth. Older children may ingest animal droppings, sand, insects, leaves, or pebbles, wood, glue, and even urine and feces.

Some researchers allege that pica may be associated with iron and zinc deficiencies. Others claim that mental retardation, poverty, poor mother-child relationship, neglect, deficient sensorial stimulations, and psychosis may all play a part in such bizarre eating habits.

Obviously, there may be health complications caused by the ingested substance, such as intestinal obstruction from hair, parasitic infestations from excrements, and even lead intoxication and subsequent brain damage and mental retardation from plaster and paint.

A caseworker requested a psychiatric evaluation of Kevin, two years old and his mother. "A physician reported that Kevin has physical and mental impairment caused by high levels of lead due to his eating plaster and old paint from the walls around his crib," said the caseworker.

A judge charged Kevin's mother with neglect of him and his older five siblings and requested a comprehensive, physical, psychosocial and psychiatric evaluation.

Kevin, his siblings, and their single mother lived in two small and deteriorated rooms in a rural area. His mother had been depressed and poorly nourished even before she became pregnant with Kevin. She recognized her difficulties in supervising and in taking good care of her children, especially Kevin, who had been left alone on the bare floor most of the time, while she struggled with her daily obligations and her untreated depressive symptoms.

Treatment consisted of the following: medical treatment of Kevin's high levels of lead and his undernourishment; medical treatment of his mother's depressive symptoms with antidepressant medication and individual and group psychosocial therapies; and caseworker supervision of his mother's compliance with prescribed parenting skills training.

Six months later, Kevin's physical, mental, and social functionings were improving, while his mother's depressive symptoms were controlled and her ability to take care of Kevin and her other children improved. The judge dropped the charges of child neglect pending against her.

Anorexia Nervosa

A more common and more serious eating disorder is Anorexia Nervosa, which today has become a real and serious problem for many, especially adolescent girls. Along with bulimia, Anorexia Nervosa has become a dangerous health threat.

As Attention Hyperactivity Deficit Disorder [Chapter 2] is mainly a disorder of males, Anorexia Nervosa is mainly a disorder of females. Study after study reports that many girls in junior high school (eleven to fourteen years of age) are dissatisfied with their body image, claiming that they are too fat. Girls as young as seven and eight are now going on diets because they see themselves as "overweight."

Some researchers theorize that anorexia appears to be a reaction to issues of dependency and independence and/or social/sexual functioning in adolescents and young adults. Others claim that Anorexia Netrosa reflects issues of personal and interpersonal control.

Anorexia Nervosa has been associated with hormonal and central nervous system illnesses; it has also been associated with self-identity, obsessive-compulsive, depressive and anxious disorders; with familial and other interpersonal conflicts; and with imitation of societal fads, especially those of model-like thinness. The disorder frequently begins around puberty, usually in a girl who has had uneventful growth and development. It can continue through adulthood.

Anorexia Nervosa manifests itself through self-imposed loss of weight by refusing to eat even when hungry, or by using laxatives, diuretics, and diet pills. The teenager has an obsession about being fat while actually thin or even emaciated, and exhibits a compulsive behavior about the preparation of food, perceiving certain foods as "good" or "bad." Irregular or absent menses often appear.

Because Anorexia Nervosa can become life threatening, parents need to consult with pediatricians, child psychiatrists, other physicians, and other professionals who are familiar with treatment of this disorder as soon as their youngster shows any early symptoms of Anorexia Nervosa -- including exaggerated physical exercise and weight reducing diet and/or a rapid weight loss for no apparent reason, or a lack of menses.

Bulimia Nervosa

Bulimia, or voracious appetite, is a symptom associated with many conditions including obesity. However, Bulimia Nervosa is a syndrome that usually, becomes apparent in adolescence or in early adult life and is more common in females than in males. The specific cause of Bulimia Nervosa is unknown, but some researchers speculate as to its possible association with depression, because bulimia sometimes improves with antidepressant medications.

The most common behavioral symptoms of bulimia are uncontrollable repetitive gorging, self-induced vomiting, diarrhea, and strict weight reducing diet, fasting, or excessive physical exercise, and obsession about weight and body shape.

The youngster with bulimia has episodes of binging/ purging behavior and is embarrassed about it. In addition, the gastric acid present in the repetitive vomiting may eat away the enamel of the teeth causing dental problems, while the repetitive diarrhea and vomiting may lead to starvation and related metabolic disturbances, such as dehydration, cardiac arrythmia and eventually death. Professional treatment is recommended for bulimia.

The bulimic symptoms of Caroline, introduced at the beginning of this chapter, improved progressively with individual and group psychotherapy, and with educational guidance as to eating habits, nutrition, and physical exercise. After six months of therapy, Caroline was free of bulimic, depressive, and anxious symptoms, had adapted to living at her college and away from her family and friends, and demanded less from herself and others. She accepted her shortcomings and felt happier with herself.

CHAPTER 4

Normal Anxiety

Allan's parents are upset because every time they want to leave him with a baby-sitter, he clings to his mother, crying, "Don't leave me, Mom." Does his behavior indicate that something is wrong with him? If Allan is eighteen months old, probably not, because at this age fear of separation from one or both parents is a normal type of separation anxiety that usually fades away if appropriately handled. If Allan is eight years old, then certainly his parents need to look for the reasons for his anxiety. In this chapter, I will examine normal anxiety in children and adolescents, how to relieve it, and when it may be associated with other serious problems.

Anxiety is the feeling of scattered apprehension and a sensation of impending danger. It helps us to mobilize our coping skills when there is any sign of a personal threat. However, when anxiety interferes with a child's normal behavior, the youngster and his or her parents need to look for its causes and its relief.

Infants

Even *infants* can react with diverse anxious behaviors when their basic needs for survival, physical comfort, or interpersonal security are not provided. Since infants lack language skills, they communicate their anxiety in a number of ways. Parents should look for these signs:

SYMPTOMS OF INFANTS' NORMAL ANXIETY
- excessive perspiration, decreased or increased appetite, regurgitation, diarrhea, frequent urination, and restless sleep
- a watchful or strained expression on their face
- tenseness in their neck, fists, and extremities
- high-pitched crying

Infants can also become anxious when they are startled by bright lights, loud sounds, or when they are moved into uncomfortable positions, as any too fond relative discovers while awkwardly trying to hold a new baby. When their mother is absent or when a stranger is present, some infants react with howls of displeasure.

Babies react with anxiety when they are uncomfortable -- hungry, sleepless, tired, cold, hot, soiled, or wet. Perceptive parents soon learn to interpret their infant's way of communicating discomfort and often even know from the sound of the child's cry what the problem is.

When you as a parent or parental surrogate act quickly to relieve distress, an infant's anxiety is usually transitory and does not leave permanent consequences. It is only when anxious reactions are ignored that they may lead to chronic irritability and fearfulness.

What can you as parents do to help your infant with anxious reactions? The first step is to recognize anxious behavior and identify its causes. Then, keep your baby clean, well fed, and warm. Maximize physical contact and provide him or her with blankets, soft pillows, dolls and toys, soft light, and low volume music, especially during your brief absences.

Holding, talking to, playing with, and caressing your baby, and expressing concern and providing affectionate care implant an early sense of personal self-worth, and the foundation for healthy interpersonal relationships.

Toddlers

Toddlers also have "reactive anxiety," a catchall phrase for everything from worries about situations insignificant to most children of a similar age to fears of the darkness, storms, animals, monsters, loud noises, and even ghosts. Reactive anxiety can also come from feelings of deprivation when sharing a parent with siblings, especially a newborn. It may manifest itself as fear of retaliation from parents or others after misbehaving, or even an usually groundless fear of losing a parent or loved family members due to their illnesses or absences.

Toddlers--like infants--cannot label feelings (sadness, fear, anger) but communicate mainly through their behavior. They express anxiety through a combination of the following symptoms:

SYMPTOMS OF TODDLERS' NORMAL ANXIETY

- general malaise, weakness, poor appetite, nausea, vomiting, abdominal discomfort, insomnia, or restless sleep with dreams or nightmares
- ideas of abandonment or deprivation
- anger against an absent or neglectful caregiver
- repetitive rituals, such as checking often for the mother's presence
- increasing requests for attention and affection, and overdependency on a parent or surrogate

Usually, reactive anxiety in toddlers is transitory and without negative consequences when the distress is alleviated and the cause eliminated or at least modified. But if not, then anxious behavior may become a repetitive and habitual way to react. For instance, leaving a toddler alone for prolonged periods of time, and harshly criticizing and punishing him or her for expressing fear of being abandoned may lead to future separation anxiety disorder and habitual uneasy or hostile reactions toward people in an authority position.

It would be easy for a parent to ridicule such reactive anxieties in a young child. But to do so, not only would be doing an injustice to the child, but would make it more difficult for you to deal with an increasingly anxious youngster. Instead, observe carefully your toddler's verbal and nonverbal communications. In particular, listen carefully for any indication of the child's fear of being neglected by you or by another significant person in his or her life. Often this is expressed as a fear or uneasiness about strangers and unknown places. Tell your toddler that you believe the fear is real to him or her, even if you feel that it is unfounded. Reassure your child with tender words and hugs, which emphasizes your protection and love.

Imagine yourself feeling neglected and think about what might help you in such a situation. Then apply that knowledge and understanding to help your youngster. Use empathy while asking your son or daughter to explain his or her thoughts, ideas, worries, and feelings. Often these can be identified through his or her drawings or play. Spend sufficient time with your child to build his or her self-esteem. Provide reassurance that you will help to relieve the anxieties and fears that have produced the problems and will eliminate the causes.

If your efforts prove ineffective, then it is time to consult a professional, preferably one experienced in the treatment of anxiety in preschool children, who can help pinpoint the cause of your toddler's normal anxiety and determine a method of treatment.

Elementary School Age Children

Elementary school age children exhibit normal anxiety through a mixture of emotional, physical, and behavioral signs and symptoms. However, because they are older, they also show it by disruptive and mischievous actions and by breaking rules in the community and at home and school. Their emotional and cognitive problems are also more sophisticated, ranging from fear of bodily injury to fears about gangs, and may include actual physical, mental, and sexual abuse. They may feel self-imposed pressure about their performance in school or excessive demands from parents, friends, teachers, and coaches.

Normal anxiety in elementary school-age children is usually of short duration and fades away when the cause is eliminated, when parents and teachers help the youngster face his or her fears. However, if the child's anxiety is ignored, or if the child is ridiculed, criticized, or punished, then anxious reactions may become repetitive and habitual, disturbing the child's life at home, in school, and in other activities.

What strategies can you use to help your elementary school-age child with reactive anxiety? You can encourage him or her to openly express concerns, worries, and fears. Restate the problem to make sure you really understand what your youngster is saying, and communicate your understanding. Then, discuss together with your child and others involved in the situation what each of you can do to eliminate, alleviate, or just help your child to live with the problem in the least painful manner.

If your child does not respond to your concerned and affectionate help, then you need to consult a professional who specializes in behavioral problems for this age group. Many elementary schools have nurses, social workers, psychologists, and counselors, who assist students and their families.

Teenagers

As *teenagers* go through physical, cognitive, social, and spiritual changes at a rapid rate, some have concerns, worries, and normal anxious reactions to such transformation. Boys may have diverse anxieties about normal physical and other characteristics of male puberty such as change of voice pitch, acne, facial hair growth, muscular development, enlargement of the penis and testes, sleep emission of semen ("wet dreams"), spontaneous or provoked erections, masturbation, sexual desires.

Girls may be normally anxious about the normal physical and other characteristics of female puberty such as enlargement of the breasts and hips, acne, first and subsequent menstruations, increased height, clitoral sensations, masturbation, and sexual desires.

At this age, some teenage boys and girls may exhibit normal anxiety about sexual activity, often wondering if they "should have done it or not," if it is normal or "weird" to have physically felt a need to do "it," or if it is right or wrong to do what they perceive their friends to be accomplishing sexually. This behavior for the age group is so familiar that dozens of famous books and movies have been based on these adolescent sexual awakenings, as adult authors look back on their high school days.

In Appendix B, I explain the reasons for these adolescent concerns in more detail. As with the other age groups, anxious reactions in this age group are usually mild and brief. If, however, the anxiety continues, it can lead to physical dysfunctions and illnesses, depression, impaired interpersonal relationships, difficulty in school and other activities, and socially deviant actions.

What strategies can you use to help prevent unhealthy anxiety in your young teenager? First of all, increase your empathy by learning about the unique traits and concerns of teenagers. Provide your son or daughter with this type of information. Explain that feelings of irritability, boredom, frustration, anger, and even anxiety and sadness are normal in appropriate circumstances. Talk to your youngster's teachers and listen to their suggestions; work together with them in helping your teenager.

Be supportive, loving, and honest with your son or daughter. Such strategies may not cure all reactive anxieties, but will help to keep them at a minimum.

No matter what the age of the person, diverse degrees of anxiety develop when the individual experiences physical illnesses and psychological conflicts as a threat to personal well being and security. Anyone who has been seriously ill or has other significant problems knows that fears about the outcome can lead to anxiety. Conscious and unrecognized emotions and thoughts such as hostility, anger, sadness, worries, guilt, obsessions, compulsions, and distrust may cause apprehension that is interpreted as a fear of personal danger.

Social problems also can cause a diverse degree of anxiety in children and adolescents. Conflictual relationships with parents, relatives, friends, and teachers are such a source. Learning disabilities can also lead to anxiety. Alcohol and other drugs cause anxious symptoms. And not less important, conflicts about faith can also cause diverse anxiety.

In fact, for some people, any situation that is interpreted as a personal threat triggers diverse reactive anxieties. However, when these anxieties become a customary way of reacting to diverse situations, then they are called anxiety *disorders*.

CHAPTER 5

Anxiety Disorders

Anxiety disorders may result from abnormal brain neurotransmitters (the chemical messengers between brain cells), hormone imbalances, learned behavior from parents and other significant people, and even inherited vulnerability or predisposition. In this chapter, I will discuss how to recognize abnormal anxiety or anxiety disorders, and how the youngster, the parents, or professionals can relieve these disorders.

Anxiety disorders manifest themselves with similar physical, emotional, reasoning, and behavioral symptoms such as those of the normal anxiety reactions discussed earlier. However, they are characterized by chronic maladaptive patterns of behavior leading to ongoing dysfunctions in the youngster's life.

The physical, psychological, social and spiritual stresses causing anxiety are interrelated. For instance, a child with diabetes (physical) may react with poor self-esteem (psychological) and isolation from his or her friends (social). Likewise, an adolescent with family problems (social) may have nightmares and headaches (physical), and react with doubts about his or her religion (spiritual).

Under the general heading of anxiety disorders, there are some specific to children and adolescents, which are listed below.

Separation Anxiety Disorder in a Child

Peter was eleven years old when his mother brought him to the pediatrician. "My husband and I have done everything we know to help our son," she said. "Instead of getting better he is getting worse; he complains of pains in his head and stomach, doesn't want to eat, is nauseated, and lately has been vomiting. He dreams about him or me getting sick, kidnapped or injured. He insists on being with me constantly. He cries easily and at times refuses to go to school or to be left alone even for short time."

Peter would often tell his mother that he didn't want to go to school because his teacher and the other students picked on him. He frequently would ask to sleep with his mother and constantly asked about her health.

The pediatrician determined quickly that Peter's problems were not caused by any physical illness. However, the pediatrician discovered that Peter's problems began six months previously, after he heard his parents threatening each other with divorce and arguing over who would have custody of him and his younger brother and sister. The doctor explained that Peter's symptoms seemed to be his way of reacting to his parents' problems and would be best addressed by a child psychiatrist.

The child or adolescent with separation anxiety disorder may, like Peter, develop chronic physical, emotional, reasoning, and behavioral symptoms, and difficulties in school, sports, and other activities.

This disorder is defined as severe anxious manifestations developed either in anticipation of or after a separation from a person to whom the child or adolescent is emotionally attached.

Young children usually express fears of losing parental love or support with physical symptoms combined with unrealistic and persistent fears of some terrible event happening. They refuse to be alone and cling to the person they fear losing.

When facing separation from someone they care about and lacking family support, some adolescents may seek extrafamilial security in school, or athletic, or aesthetic activities. Some may seek such protection in charismatic cults. Still others may search for it in antisocial cults or gangs, in the use of alcohol and other addictive drugs, and in individual or group criminal acts.

If something is done to alleviate the distress and to eliminate or at least reduce its cause, anxious reactions to separations are transitory. But if they are ignored, then these behavior patterns may become a customary way for a youngster to act, which impairs his or her functioning--a separation anxiety disorder.

As a parent, you can help your children by showing ongoing affectionate care, support, and respect for their concerns, worries, and fears about separation, and by providing for their physical, psychological, social, and spiritual needs.

Separation anxiety disorder can be prevented or at least minimized by explaining to your child and adolescent the reasons for the separation early and clearly; by clarifying misconceptions; by encouraging expression of feelings and fears of abandonment; and by helping to eliminate fantasies about separation. Nevertheless, if these interventions are not sufficient, then, professional help is needed to help the child and teach the parents new ways of coping with the actual or anticipated separation.

Children and adolescents with separation anxiety disorders can help themselves and should be encouraged to do so. They need to be persuaded to talk openly to their parents or any other trusted person about their concerns and fears about separation. They need to make an effort to understand the realities of the separation and try to deal with it by asking their parents for advice, support, or professional help.

Overanxious Disorder

Joan, who is 16 years old, complained that for the past eight months, she was frequently uneasy, irritable, unable to sleep, had recurring headaches, and was worried about her performance in school and extracurricular activities.

Her mother is a renowned architect, a talented pianist, and published novelist. Her father is a successful attorney, editor for his professional journal, and a good violinist. They had programmed Joan's daily activities since her birth. When she was three years old, they signed her up in classes to "help her to be the best among her peers." Since age six, she has been an A student. She plays the violin, and is the captain of her school's tennis team. She is also the editor of her school newspaper, and recently became a guest columnist for a suburban newspaper.

Physical examination and laboratory tests proved negative for any physical illness that might be causing her symptoms. However, a psychiatric examination revealed an adolescent with overanxious disorder associated with exaggerated and compulsive demands from herself and her parents to achieve excellence in increasing activities -- she was reacting to this pressure with ongoing anxious behaviors.

This type of overanxious disorder is a state of almost constant apprehension and worry. When manifested for brief periods and when related to a specific difficulty, this behavior is a normal reaction of many adolescents. However, such behavior is part of an overanxious disorder when it becomes a habit pattern for at least six months and is difficult to control. As in Joan's case, the disorder may manifest itself in a mixture of generalized apprehension or restlessness, fatigue, inability to concentrate, and other problems (headaches, hair pulling, nail biting) for which there is no demonstrable physical cause.

When expectations or demands, whether self-imposed or from parents, teachers, coaches, exceed a youngster's abilities, he or she becomes overstressed and overreacts with a combination of physical symptoms, self-consciousness, poor self-esteem, and fear of criticism and failure, resulting in worries and apprehension about past, present and future performances.

Overanxious reactions seem to be more common in children and adolescents with highly competitive, compulsive, and anxious parents.

If you are a child or teenager with overanxious disorder, you can help yourself by trying to identify the specific causes of your excessive anxious reactions, by working to eliminate self-imposed unrealistic expectations, and by asking your parents and others not to put exaggerated demands upon you.

As parents, you can help your children with overanxious disorder by identifying and eliminating, or at least diminishing, unreasonable performance expectations you are placing on your youngsters and by asking teachers and others to do the same. In other words, do not try to gain your own emotional and other needs through your children. Accept reasonable performances as praiseworthy and view each achievement according to your youngster's realistic capacities.

General Self-Help Strategies to Resolve or Alleviate Anxiety Disorders

As a child or adolescent you depend on your parents or parental substitutes to take care of your basic (physical, emotional, cognitive, social, and spiritual) needs. However, you will feel more secure and proud of yourself when you take personal responsibility for trying to solve your problems - always with the understanding that your age and experience may limit how much you can do.

For instance, if you are experiencing a mixture of symptoms and signs of anxiety, you can help yourself by doing what you know has helped you before and/or by using some of the following four groups of self-help strategies.

I. Recognize the symptoms and signs of your anxiety.

The first strategy in helping yourself is to become aware of the mixture of physical, emotional, reasoning, and behavioral problems that characterize anxiety by answering the following questions:

1. Do you have a mixture of the physical symptoms of anxiety discussed previously in this chapter?
   A. Do you have illnesses that seem to have no physical cause?
   B. Do you feel restless, frightened, and unable to relax?
   C. Do you think something bad is going to happen to you or someone you care about?
   D. Do you put unrealistic demands on yourself?
   E. Are your parents, teachers, coaches, friends, and others putting unrealistic demands on you?
   F. Do you feel uneasy or impatient with people?
   G. Do you feel remorseful, ashamed, or guilty?
   H. Do you feel insecure, inferior, or worthless?
   I. Do you feel unhappy even after reaching your aspirations and receiving praise from others?

2. Do you exhibit the following behavioral problems?
    A. Are you uneasy around people, even your family and friends? Do you avoid meeting people, or going out of the house or to school?
    B. Do you find yourself overreacting to situations?
    C. Do you act in repetitive or ritualistic ways?
    D. Do you seek attention frequently, and are impatient with those around you?

II. After recognizing the symptoms of your anxiety, try to identify the specific problems that trigger your anxiety.

1. When, where and why do you have physical symptoms of anxiety?
2. When, where and why do you feel anger, sadness, guilt, apprehension, restlessness, unhappiness or fear?
3. When, where, and why do you feel insecure, inferior, or worthless?
4. When, where, with whom, and why do you feel uneasy, tense, or anxious?
5. When, where, and why do you have fears of eternal punishment?

III. Eliminate or decrease the physical, psychological, social, and spiritual cause of anxiety.

1. To eliminate or decrease physical causes of anxiety, do the following:
    A. Avoid food and substances that produce apprehension (nicotine, alcoholic beverages and other addicting drugs, and excessive coffee, tea, sodas, and artificial sweeteners).
    B. Ask your parents, grandparents, aunts, uncles, older siblings, and other trusted persons for advice about your physical symptoms.
    C. If your health permits, do physical exercise as often as possible.

2. To eliminate or reduce emotional and cognitive causes of anxiety, ask your parents and other trusted relatives and friends to help you whenever you feel anxious or fearful. Ask your parents and other relatives, peers, teachers, coaches and others not to put you into stressful situations.

3. To eliminate or decrease social causes of anxieties, avoid involvement with persons involved in dangerous and or unlawful acts.

4. To eliminate or reduce spiritual causes of anxiety, ask your parents or spiritual counselor for help.

IV. If these methods are unsuccessful, and you still feel anxious, ask your parents to seek professional help.

As a parent, you can help resolve or alleviate the anxiety disorders of your youngsters by first recognizing their anxious symptoms, and then by identifying their causes, and finally, by helping to eliminate or diminish the causes of the anxiety.

- Listen attentively to your son's or daughter's concerns, worries, and fears about health problems.
- Does he or she have any demonstrable or imagined physical problem that is alarming?
- When, where, and why does he or she exhibit symptoms of anxiety?
- When, where, and why does your child feel useless, unloved by you and other significant persons, or disliked or discriminated against by family, friends, teachers, coaches?
- When, where, and why does your youngster express unfounded conviction of impending tragedy?
- When, where, and why does he or she avoid situations or show attention seeking, compulsive, or panicky behaviors?
- Can you recall any unusual or specific incident that might have triggered this anxiety?

After you identify at least some of the causes of your youngster's anxiety, you can try to help to eliminate or at least modify it. One way to do that is by trying the following strategies:

- Listen to your youngster with genuine attention, concern and a desire to help.
- Emphasize to your child that minimal differences in bodily features are normal.
- Reassure your child that differences in ability to learn a particular subject are normal.
- Educate him or her about the normal physical, educational, behavioral, cultural, spiritual, and social similarities and differences among all age groups.
- Provide affectionate care and reassurance to help to eliminate his or her unfounded feelings of being unloved or neglected by you and your spouse. However, if your youngster's feelings are a reality, admit that and explain your feelings about and plans to correct the situation.
- Find ways to work together with your son or daughter and his or her educators to eliminate or reduce any problems in educational, athletic, social, and other activities.
- Advise him or her to talk to a religious counselor about unresolved religious conflicts and/or fear of divine punishment.
- If necessary, seek professional help.

If help provided by parents, teachers, coaches, and others is not successful, then, seek professional help. Obtaining professional help, whether from a child psychiatrist, psychologist, social worker, or spiritual counselor, is not an admission of blame for your youngster's anxiety or an inability to help your son or daughter, but instead a demonstration of your love and concern. Often, anxiety disorders are caused by problems that are so much a part of the family's structure and interactions, that it takes a professional's neutrality, training, and experience to pinpoint the cause and recommend pertinent therapies.

Take advantage of programs offered by schools, communities, and churches and synagogues to help alleviate the anxiety of your child or adolescent, and the stress that such a problem puts on you and your family.

CHAPTER 6

Panic Disorder

Seventeen year old Maria reported sudden episodes of apprehension, sweating, nausea, chest pressure, lightheadness and fearfulness. Her symptoms began with delayed monthly menstrual periods six months previously. A physical examination showed nothing wrong. A cardiology examination did not confirm a suspected mitral valve prolapse of the heart. Her gynecological examination was normal. However, everyone who examined her noted that she seemed to be too tense, too worried, too impatient, and especially too fearful.

Maria's symptoms were identified as panic attacks precipitated by her fears of pregnancy. Since age 16, she has had sexual intercourse with her boyfriend "only during the safe days between my periods." She had had an abortion seven months ago. "I knew counting the days is not really safe, but I never thought that [pregnancy] would happen to me. I had to get rid of it." Since her abortion, she has continued to have unprotected sex in the same way "except during the days of my ovulation" and with the same attitude "that [pregnancy] will not happen to me, again."

After three months of using birth control method recommended by her gynecologist, and psychotropic medications and weekly sessions of psychotherapy, her menstrual periods became regular and her panic attacks became progressively less frequent and less intense.

Panic disorder is a type of anxiety disorder. It is characterized by sudden, repetitive, uncontrollable panic attacks. The individual may experience a panic attack anywhere or under certain circumstances. *Panic disorder with agoraphobia* refers to anxiety about being in a place or in a situation from which escape may be difficult or embarrassing or in which help may not be available. For instance, an individual with panic disorder with agoraphobia suddenly reacts with panic while he or she is in a crowd, waiting in line, on an elevator, or while traveling in a automobile, bus, train, or airplane. Thus, someone with panic disorder with agoraphobia usually avoids places or situations where he or she might have such panic attacks. Panic disorder is not uncommon in adolescents and in primary school age children, especially those with a history of depression or separation from or loss of a parent or other meaningful person.

Studies reveal that young people who have panic attacks, with or without agoraphobia, frequently have one or both parents who exhibit similar symptoms. Panic disorder runs in some families, especially in immediate relatives of patients and in monozygotic twins. Many individuals with such attacks seem to have a constitutional predisposition to them and to have learned panicky reactions.

As required by her son's preschool director, the mother of Ramoncito consulted me because "... my son refuses to be at his preschool. He refuses to visit his friends in their homes and insists they come to our home. When my husband or I insist that he stays at the school, like the other children do, he suddenly cries, feels dizzy, and complains of stomach ache, chest pressure, difficulty in breathing, or a headache and at times he vomits . . . he cries . . . he is afraid."

Ramoncito was a healthy four year old. He developed the above symptoms after he started school two months before. He exhibited symptoms every time his mother tried to leave him at school or at his friend's home. "He has never allowed me to leave him in his class with his teacher and other children. I have to stay with him either inside his classroom or outside the door as long as he could see me," said his mother. "People tell me to take him inside of the classroom and leave him there, like other parents do. At times I think he will have problems when he starts kindergarten and later on, but, I don't want to force him. I think he is not ready to stay without me. The teacher just goes along with it. He seems to need me a lot," said his mother. She showed a rather calm acceptance of her son's behavior.

"I don't want my mommy to leave me alone. I am afraid and I feel sick when she goes away from me," said Ramoncito. As he developed some trust in me, he told me, "I am afraid that my mommy would not come back. I am afraid something bad would happen to me. I am afraid something bad would happen to my mommy."

During the previous eight months his mother had been hospitalized four times to evaluate her illnesses. "My internist and cardiologist told me I was stressed-out," said his mother. During the same period of time Ramoncito's father worked hard, arriving home late at night and leaving home early in the morning. "My doctors also told me that I'm too stressed," said his father.

Ramoncito's parents were also having marital problems and he and his three younger siblings witnessed their ongoing and mutually disrespectful criticism and insults. His brother and sister who were closest to him in age were showing behavioral problems as well.

Ramoncito was experiencing a mixture of panic disorder, separation anxiety disorder, and agoraphobia.

How a Child or Adolescent Can Help Stop Panic Attacks

If you suffer from panic attacks, you can help yourself by becoming aware of the causes of your reaction and by doing something about it. Begin by answering some of the following questions:

- When do you feel panicky? When you are alone? Accompanied by someone you don't like or don't want to be with?
- Where do you feel panicky? Is there any special place or situation that provokes a panic attack?
- What are your feelings immediately before you become fearful? What are you thinking about immediately before you feel afraid?
- What are your feelings and thoughts during the panic attack?

As you try to understand why you react with panic, you also need to talk with your parents, relatives, teacher, or friends about what is bothering you and your fears, and to ask them for advice.

How Parents Can Help Stop Their Youngster's Panic Attacks

As a parent, you can help your child or adolescent deal with panic disorder by listening with empathy, and paying close attention to his or her answers to the questions listed above. In addition, consider the following questions. Your accurate answers will help you to identify the causes of your son's or daughter's panic.

- Do you often react with unrealistic worries, fear, or panic?
- Does anyone else close to your child or adolescent have a panic disorder?
- What else might contribute to your son's or daughter's panic reactions? Has there been a mishandled separation, deprivation, or threat?

If you answered yes to the above questions, you can help your youngster by trying the following?

- Show ongoing and empathetic understanding and reassurance to your youngster. Encourage him or her to relax and face problems one at a time.
- Become motivated to participate with your youngster in individual and family counseling and other therapies to eliminate or at least reduce the causes of your son's or daughter's panic disorder.

If the above self help methods are not effective, then, professional consultation is recommended.

Repetitive panic attacks, although often hard to understand, should be taken seriously since these may lead to physical dysfunctions and emotional and interpersonal problems.

CHAPTER 7

Phobic Disorders

Sandra, seven years old, was referred by her school counselor because she refused to use the closet students used to store their belongings. She would say she was dizzy and nauseated, and screamed whenever the teacher urged her to use the classroom closet.

Her mother said that recently, Sandra had become afraid of closets at home as well and was reacting the same way she did at school.

During therapy, Sandra revealed that her phobia of closets had started after her mother found her masturbating and angrily slapped her face and right hand, locked her up for hours in a closet without light, and told her, "You are a pervert. You should not play with your pussy, that is evil. You better stop doing that because if you do it again, I will put you away."

As can be seen by Sandra's reactions, a specific phobia is an intense and persistent fear of an object or a situation that has become a symbol of threat or conflict. A child or an adolescent either avoids or endures with dread the place or situation causing the fear. Many younger children express anxiety through tantrums, crying, clinging or immobilization. They do not identify fear as intense or unreasonable and seldom identify a phobia to a specific object or situation. However, they often have transitory fear of specific animals and objects. Many older children and adolescents usually recognize the dread as irrational or excessive, and feel "stupid," "weird," embarrassed, or humiliated about it.

However, like Sandra, most children and teenagers are not aware of their conflictual thoughts and feelings causing their feared object or situation. For instance, it took Sandra about four months of weekly therapy sessions to become aware of her devastating "... fear of being abandoned by my mother for being a bad girl," as she said, terrified.

Phobic disorders interfere with the youngster's functioning at home, school or somewhere else. Fear of spirits, magic or witchcraft, is present in many cultures. However, it becomes a specific phobia when the fear becomes intense and persistent and causes distress or dysfunctions.

At the present time, there is no known specific cause of phobic disorder. Theories of its etiology range from genetic and physical to intrapersonal and interpersonal factors. Some specific phobias run in the immediate family of individuals with such disorder, -- for example, an intense and persistent fear of blood that causes fainting.

As with any anxious behavior, youngsters may learn to react in a phobic manner from parents, relatives, and friends. Often they develop specific phobias after certain threats. A mother might say, "If you don't do what I tell you, I will ask the doctor to give you a shot." This not only can give the child a phobia about doctors, but can make the mother's life miserable every time she tries to get her child in for treatment. Threats such as, "If you don't eat the whole thing, a monster will get you while you are asleep," may cause a child to fear sleep. These fears of needles or sleep become symbolic of the interpersonal threat or conflict that originated it.

Strategies the Young Person Can Use to Handle Phobias

- Identify the specific object, animal, or situation that you fear a lot.
- Try to remember the first time you were afraid of it and what you did about that fear.
- Did you think you were going to be injured? Did someone frighten you by threatening you with that object or situation?
- Have you seen someone reacting with fear to anything? Does anyone in your family have fears like yours?

Once you recognize that what you fear is not really dangerous, make an effort to eliminate your belief of danger and try to control your anxiety. If that does not relieve your specific fear, then, ask your parents or someone you trust to help you.

How Parents Can Help Their Youngster with Phobic Disorder

- Determine whether your son or daughter learned to react with fear from you, another relative, or someone else close to him or her.
- Accept his or her dread, no matter how irrational it may seem to you, without criticism or other negative reactions.
- Accompany your child to deal with the object or situation that is causing the phobia for brief periods of time, always reassuring him or her that eventually the dread will diminish and disappear. If this is handled well, then progressive and reassuring exposure to the fear will help to eliminate the phobia. If this technique is too threatening to your youngster, then do not force him or her to continue with it. Wait until he or she is ready for it.
- Avoid the use of force, bargains, blackmail, or other types of manipulation to try to end the phobic behavior.
- Consult professionals for help if the above techniques do not work or if you are uncomfortable using them.

The fear of an object or a situation may seem to be unfounded, silly, or irrational to the youngster who experiences it or to others. However, because such phobic disorder is distressful to him or her, it may cause emotional, educational, and interpersonal problems, and it needs to be resolved by the youngster with or without help of parents and relatives. If the parents and the youngster's efforts are not effective, professional elp is recommended.

CHAPTER 8

Posttraumatic Stress Disorder

When George heard the bell of the entrance door of his home, he opened it. A man, with sunglasses hiding his eyes and with a cloth covering the rest of his face, asked to see George's father and then shot him while George looked on. The father remained in coma and received medical and surgical treatments for three weeks in the intensive care unit of a university hospital.

As described by his mother, since the day his father was shot, seven year old George had had daily repetitive episodes of unusual behavior: "He wears a red cloth covering his face below his sunglasses, grabs a toy pistol, runs throughout the house, avoiding the front door, while repeating, 'Good morning, I need to speak with your father. Dad, a man needs you. Bang, bang, bang, oh, Dad!'" George would then shoot his toy pistol three times, moving his head up, down, to the left, to the right and to the back, breathing heavily and rapidly. He would then repeat the whole scenario over and over again, until he became exhausted and would fall into deep sleep.

George was also reacting to everyday situations with increasing panic, disorganized speech and actions, and whenever he would hear the doorbell, would become frantic. Since the tragedy, he had had nightmares related to 'the shooting of his father, as well physical and behavioral problems at home and school.

The intensity and frequency of George's posttraumatic stress disorder began to decrease after his father returned home. With medications to promote sleep and control anxiety, individual and joint sessions with him and his mother, and ongoing support from relatives and friends, he became the well-adjusted little boy he had been before this traumatic event.

Posttraumatic stress syndrome is characterized by intense fear, hopelessness, helplessness, and disorganized and agitated behavior which develops after an overwhelming negative experience.

The traumatic experience is repetitively reexperienced through a mixture of intrusive, recurrent, and distressing mental images and feelings. Behavior becomes disorganized and agitated, with nightmares and physical and mental distress. There may also be a persistent avoidance of any person or thing related to the experience.

Posttraumatic stress syndrome can develop after someone experiences a sudden serious personal injury, or is subjected to physical, sexual, and mental abuse. It can also be initiated by witnessing a sudden death, unexpected life-threatening injury, or abuse of a significant person in the youngster's life -- as happened to George.

Ways to Help Your Child or Adolescent Cope With This Disorder:

Talk to him or her openly about all the aspects related with the traumatic incident. Show empathy about his or her reactions. Try to relieve your youngster's worries, guilt, hostility, and anger with reassurances and support. Avoid criticisms and demonstrate understanding. With this disorder, you will probably have to seek medical, psychological, and even legal advice.

The conflictual thoughts, feelings, and behavior of a child or an adolescent caused by any situation experienced as a threat or injury results in repetitive and severe anxious and fearful reactions. These may lead to serious impairment of the youngster's functioning at home, school and community. The youngster needs to resolve such distress with or without help from parents, relatives and others, and often, parents need to seek medical, psychological and, if necessary, legal help.

CHAPTER 9

Sexuality

The current preoccupation with sex appeal, sexual performance ("scoring") and the increasingly serious consequences of careless sexual activities make sexual behavior and related issues crucial.

Sexuality results from a complex interaction between genetics, and prenatal and postnatal experiences. Sexuality reflects an individual's sexual identity, gender identity, sexual orientation, sexual behavior and the socially assigned roles of masculinity or femininity.

The transmission of personal traits from parents to offspring through chromosomes or carriers of DNA spirals called genes is wondrous. The chromosomes are diverse living matter in the nuclei of every human cell arranged in 23 pairs. Among these, 22 pairs determine the physical features of the father and the mother and are called autosomal chromosomes. The other pair is either an XY sex chromosome of the male or an XX sex chromosome of the female. If the X of the XY chromosome of the sperm pairs with an X of the XX chromosome present in the ovum the resultant embryo will be a female; if the Y of the XY chromosome of the sperm pairs with an X of the ovum's XX, the embryo will be a male.

In some pregnancies, two ova are simultaneously re-eased and each is fertilized by a separate sperm and they develop as dizygotic (fraternal) twins. These twins frequently have similar physical characteristics, as do any siblings, but can be the same or opposite sex and develop similar and different personality traits.

In other pregnancies one ovum is fertilized and divided into two or, much less often, into several embryos. These develop as monozygotic (paternal) siblings with identical hereditary characteristics and develop similar and different personality traits. Some may have different constitutional capabilities.

In some pregnancies, aberrations of sexual chromosomes cause congenital sexual disorders. For instance, a zygote with only one X chromosome results into an XO embryo with feminine appearance which does not secrete estrogens and after birth does not develop full femaleness or fertility *(Turner's Syndrome)*. Other deviations in the arrangement of the chromosomes X or Y may produce an XXY embryo which develops into an eunuchold "male" *(Klinefelter's syndrome)* with small testicles, large breasts, weak libido, tendencies to transvestism and other physical and personality deviations. Another abnormality can become a partially masculinized "female" *(Noonan' s syndrome)*.

No one can choose parents who give genetic traits that made a person male or female; no one can choose the growing up experiences that shaped his or sexuality; no one can choose hormonal and other physiological functions that produce sexual sensations; and no one can choose relatives, schoolmates, neighbors, and other persons whose sexuality may serve as a role model. But, every person can choose his or her sexual behavior just as every person can choose friends, food, play, TV and computer programs, and other activities.

Messages from Your Body and Culture

Some of the physiological functions that contribute to the stimulation or inhibitions of sexual sensations and activity include sex-related hormones; constriction and dilation of the veins and arteries of the genitals; the senses (sight, hearing, touch, smell, taste); and the sensation of positions and movements of the extremities and the head. In addition, the sensory nerves transmit stimuli to the brain which interprets it as pleasant or unpleasant and sends this message to arouse or inhibit the sexual response. Then the mental functions of thinking and feeling and behaving determine the choice to act or not to act sexually.

Beliefs and values influence decisions, including sexual behavior. In addition to the influences provided by physiological functions and mental imagery, sexuality is variously and highly influenced by the sexual beliefs and practices of a person's parents, siblings, other relatives, and his or her culture.

Parents have a crucial and responsible role in educating their child and adolescent about sexuality. You can educate your child or adolescent about sexuality with plain verbal and nonverbal communications according to his or her level of physical, emotional, intellectual development--and without mysterious, negative, seductive, bribing, and other manipulative attitudes. You can do that in response to his or her questions about sexual issues, or even if direct questions are not asked, in anticipation to their being asked.

You can explain, clarify and inform your youngster about his or her sexual development, how to take good care of genital areas, how to respect his or her own sexuality and the sexuality of others, how to be assertive in rejecting any sexual overtures or seductive behavior from others. Studies show that people who had meaningful familial relationships, appropriate parental and other familial models on sexuality, and received appropriate sexual education by parents or surrogates throughout childhood and adolescence have small risk for developing sexual problems. By contrast, other studies show that children with deficient familial ties, increased exposure to inappropriate sexual freedom in their parents, siblings, and relatives, deficient supervision and guidance, and with lack of or conflictual education about sexuality, have great risk for developing sexual problems.

Children and adolescents may become confused by the diverse and often contradictory issues about sexuality, particularly in a society like the U.S.A. where distinctions between popular literature and overt pornography is slim, and where constant bombardment with nudity, open heterosexual and homosexual activities, rapes, and prostitution are easily available to youngsters in their homes through television and Internet.

Your Personal Choices, Responsibility, and Sexual Behavior

As with any type of human action, people can choose sexual thoughts, feelings and behavior. Even when sexual sensations are produced exclusively by physiological functions, each person can decide what to feel and what to do or not to do about them. Personal choice regarding sexual thoughts, feelings, and behavior reflects individual beliefs about physical, interpersonal, religious, social, and legal concepts related to sexual issues.

People can ignore, modify, or act upon their sexual thoughts or feelings, and the choices involve personal responsibility. If a person has constant sexual thoughts and feelings, and masturbates as frequently as possible, he or she may develop an obsessive compulsive disorder about sexuality. This may interfere with his or her educational, athletic, and other activities and even cause related emotional problems, all of which may require professional help.

If a person has hetero- or homosexual intercourse with an unknown person without protection, this is a manifestation of deficient personal responsibility since he or she increases the risk of acquiring AIDS or other sexually transmitted diseases, or transmitting these diseases to a partner. Heterosexual intercourse without protection brings with it the risk of conceiving a child, who if unwanted, may become the cause of many problems.

Every individual is accountable for either personal or interpersonal and social complications resulting from his or her sexual activities. Alleging that "I could not help" avoiding or having sexual intercourse reflects denial of the consciously motivated activities leading to intercourse, and dismissal of personal choice and personal responsibility in doing so.

When people protest, "I do not want to smoke, drink, use illicit drugs, or be sexually promiscuous . . . I want to avoid it... but, I cannot help myself," what they are saying is what they wish others to believe, not what they really intended to do all along. In fact, the real issue is that whatever people do or do not do results from personal choice based on personal motivations, regardless of protests to the contrary.

Sexually-Transmitted Diseases

Any sexually active person, regardless of age, may become infected by any of the following diseases transmitted through unprotected, and sometimes even protected, sexual activities.

<u>Gonorrhea</u>

Charlie, twelve years old, developed burning and at times pain on urination and a pus-like discharge from the penis two weeks after having had unprotected sexual intercourse. A physician diagnosed gonorrhea. Usually, symptoms of this disease appear from one to three weeks after the sexual contact.

The gonococci "Neisseria gonorrheae" is transmitted through the site of sexual contact. Thus, it may cause infection of the genitals, rectum, and mouth. The gonococci may cause arthritis and ocular infections. Men may develop gonorrheal infection of the urethra and epididymis which may lead to sterility. In women it may cause Pelvic Inflammatory Disease (PID) with infection of the Fallopian tubes which may lead to sterility.

Gonorrheal infections are common in adolescents and may appear in children and infants. Many infected individuals are asymptomatic.

<u>Syphilis</u>

One month after sexual intercourse with a stranger, Cassandra, a sixteen year old girl, developed a red skin lesion *(papule)* that became a painless ulcer *(chancre)* on the lip. Physical examination and laboratory tests diagnosed syphilis.

Chancres develop in the site of sexual contact such as the penis, vulva, uterus, anus, rectum, perineum, lips, tongue, buccal mucosa, tonsils, or fingers. Untreated syphilis may become symptomless even for many years. But eventually, serious complications can appear including skin lesions, deafness, blindness, cardiovascular and urinary lesions, and even dementia. Newborns from pregnant women with syphilis develop congenital syphilis and may die.

Genital Herpes

Sam, a fifteen year old boy, developed several painful sores on his penis and Raquel, his girlfriend, found painful pimples on her vulva. They had herpes sores. These are transmitted through skin-to-skin contact. The individual can develop painful blisters on the genitals, the anus, the rectum, the womb, the lips, or the extremities. The infection tends to recur.

An individual may carry the virus for years before developing sores or other symptoms. In the U.S.A., over thirty million persons are infected with herpes, but many don't know it. Genital Herpes can cause brain damage or death o newborns. The virus can also spread and cause infection of the brain, medulla, peripheral nerves, autonomic nervous system, skin, joints, liver, and lungs.

Genital Warts

After one to six months from the time of sexual contact, warts develop in the genitals, the anus, the rectum, and the uterus. Genital warts have been associated with cancer of the uterine cervix and are common in the U.S.A.

Chlamydia

This is another infection caused by a bacteria spread through sexual contact. In the U.S.A., over four million persons develop chlamydia each year. Usually symptoms appear seven to twenty-one days after sexual contact. In males, they include painful urination and penile discharge. In females, the symptoms include vaginal discharge, bleeding, and painful urination. Most women are asymptomatic unless the infection causes Pelvic Inflammatory Disease *(PID)*.

The responsible organism of chlamydia can cause infection of the genitals in sexually active boys, girls, men and women, and of the uterus and pelvis in females. Chlamydia during pregnancy can cause infection of a newborn's eyes, lungs, and other organs, and even miscarriage.

Acquired Immunodeficiency Syndrome

Acquired Immunodeficiency Syndrome *(AIDS)* is caused by the human immunodeficiency virus *(HIV)* transmitted through sexual contact or infected needles. AIDS is a main cause of early death among teenagers, particularly blacks and Hispanics.

The HIV of a mother can be transmitted to her offspring through the placenta or through the close contact with the mother during or after birth. Many infected fetuses die as stillborn or spontaneous abortion, or are born and develop progressive encephalopathy, mental retardation, and seizures during infancy. Usually, children born infected with HIV live only a few years.

A person infected with AIDS develops skin lesions, fever, diarrhea, poor appetite, progressive emaciation, and increasing loss of immunological defenses, delirium, and eventually may die. It also leads to substance abuse, anxiety, depression, dementia, psychosis, suicide, personality disorders, and mania.

Prevention requires sexual abstinence or reliable condoms, avoidance of mucous "extragenital" contacts (e.g. lingual kissing), and the use of carefully sterilized needles.

At present, there is no cure for AIDS, but new medications and research provide future hope. Additional help is available through necessary nutritional counseling, and diverse individual, couple and group psychotherapies, religious counseling and occupational, recreational, and creative activities.

Sexually active individuals decrease the risk of infection by using condoms and by avoiding contact with infected bodily fluids and infected mucous, such as in the mouth.

Unfortunately, many sexually active teenagers may not know or may ignore and discard the fact that many sexually transmitted diseases are asymptomatic. In addition, many do not believe they can become infected, and take the dangerous risk of having sexual activities without protection.

People cannot avoid infecting each other with a sexually transmitted disease just because they trust each other. They may carry an infectious organism without knowing about it. The only real safety is to abstain from sexual contact. Even using a condom is not completely safe since it may break.

Prostitution

A large number of prostitutes are teenagers, with estimates of over one million in the U.S.A., alone. Most adolescent prostitutes are girls, but boys can be homosexual prostitutes. Studies show that most adolescent prostitutes have been abused as children or have grown up in chaotic families. A large number were raped, especially the girls. Many ran away from home and were taken advantage by pimps and users of illicit drugs.

Sexual Dysfunctions

Sexually active teenagers may develop disorders of the sexual response cycle which involves four sexual phases: desire, arousal, orgasm, and resolution. Dysfunctions in any of these phases may be symptomatic of physical, intrapersonal, or interpersonal problems. They become a clinical disorder when they cause distress to the individual. The dysfunction may be generalized or present regardless of the situations; or specific to a particular partner or situation.

Sexual Desire Dysfunctions
These are characterized by deficient or absent desire for sexual activity or by an aversion to and avoidance of genital contact with a sexual partner. In the U.S.A., it is estimated that twenty percent of persons have deficient or absent sexual desire and that it is more common in women than in men.

Sexual Arousal Dysfunctions
Females with impaired sexual excitement have persistent or recurrent failure to produce or maintain genital lubrication

throughout the sexual act. Males with impaired sexual arousal have persistent or recurrent failure to attain or maintain an erection throughout the sexual act. However, if sexual stimulation is absent or deficient in type, focus, intensity, or duration, the problems with female genital lubrication and male erection are not considered a real sexual dysfunction.

Orgasmic Dysfunctions

These are characterized by recurrent or persistent delay in or absence of orgasm after a normal sexual excitement that is adequate in type, focus, intensity, and duration. The inability to experience orgasm in males and females by coitus or masturbation is called *anorgasmia*. Males with premature ejaculation have persistent or recurrent orgasm and ejaculation before they wish to; often they ejaculate before or immediately after penile penetration.

Sexual Resolution Dysfunctions

The last phase of coitus called resolution refers to the sense of general and muscular relaxation and the experience of mental and physical satisfaction and well-being after the male and female orgasm and the male ejaculation. Usually, during this sexual phase, men do not have additional orgasm for a period of time that increases with age, whereas women are capable of having multiple orgasms without a refractory period. Males and females may develop dysphoria and headache symptomatic of dysfunction of the sexual phase of resolution.

Sexual Dysfunctions Due to General Medical Conditions

Male erectile dysfunction may be caused by genetics, nutrition, infections, parasites, or cardiovascular, renal and urologic, hepatic, pulmonary, endocrine, and neurological disorders. Other causes of male erectile problems are poisoning, surgical procedures, radiation therapy, pelvic fracture, and any severe debilitating condition. Alcohol and other addicting drugs, and prescribed and over-the-counter medications are common causes of male erectile dysfunction. Sexual pain dysfunctions in females can be caused by pelvic disorders, pelvic and genital surgery, irritation, or infections of the remnants of the hymen, vulva, vagina, uterine cervix, and endometriosis. Sclerotic plaques of the penis *(Peyronie's disease)* cause penile curvature that causes pain in males during coitus *(dyspareunia)*.

Sexual desire often decreases after major illnesses or surgery, and with the use of drugs that depress the central nervous system or decreases testosterone production. Male orgasmic dysfunction can be caused by surgery on the genitourinary tract, and by Parkinson's disease and other neurological disorders of the lumbar and sacral sections of the spinal cord. Female orgasmic dysfunction can be caused by hypothyroidism, diabetes mellitus, certain medications including some antidepressant, antianxiety, and antipsy-chotic medications.

Alcohol and other addicting substances can cause sexual dysfunction with impairment of desire, arousal, orgasm, and of resolution, and pain during coitus. Other sexual dysfunctions are: absence of pleasure during orgasm and pain during masturbation.

A female may develop recurrent or persistent genital pain before, during, or after coitus *(dyspareunia),* or involuntary muscle constriction of the outer third of the vagina with pain or anticipation of pain that interferes with the insertion of the penis and coitus *(vaginismus)*.

Treatment of Sexual Dysfunctions

The following therapies are being used singly or in combination to treat sexual problems: dual-sex therapy, behavior therapy, individual, couple and group psychotherapies, hypnotherapy, pharmacotherapy, and surgery.

Sexual Counseling

Some teenagers who are single and younger than eighteen years, are referred for therapy because they feel "nervous" or "unhappy." They confess that what they really wish is confidential guidance to resolve their sexual concerns, but insist that what they need is guidance in erotic techniques.

The therapist should advise the teenager with empathy and tact that eventually seeking parental guidance may decrease familial distrusts and tensions. But, if this is not effective, the therapist advises again with tact and empathy, that if the adolescent decides to find erotic instruction some where else it is wise to be careful and emphasizes the following initial cautions:

- Sexuality is not just erotic activities; a healthy sexuality involves a steady and caring friendship with mutual respect of individual needs, beliefs and customs; with a mutual sense of well-being; with mutual acceptance of individual differences; with mutual physical and affective attraction; with mutual tender affection and sexual expressions; and with mutual caution and responsibility to prevent distressful consequences of unprotected sexual contacts.
- For most people, the first sexual experience may be highly significant and sometimes highly distressful particularly for girls.
- Contrary to "macho" myths, a "no!" does not always mean a timid *"yes."*
- Erotic activities without a steady and mutually caring and respectful relationship usually end as physical "scoring" without any affection.
- Unprotected sexual contacts especially with an unknown and promiscuous partner pose a risk for being infected with sexually transmitted diseases.
- Having sexual intercourse with the use of condoms does not give complete protection from AIDS and other sexually transmitted diseases. These can also be transmitted through rectal and oral sexual and nonsexual contacts
- The safest way to prevent pregnancy is not to have vaginal intercourse.

- Unprotected vaginal intercourse with ejaculation outside the vagina is not absolutely safe either. It takes only one among the many spermatozoids present in just one drop of semen to produce a pregnancy.
- The rhythm method is not safe. Many females who have unprotected vaginal intercourse immediately before, during, and immediately after the menses become pregnant.
- Birth control devices (condom, birth control pills, sperm-killer compounds, intrauterine coil, and vaginal diaphragm) are not completely safe. Many women become pregnant despite their use.
- Using seductive manipulations, inappropriate persuasions, demands, threats, or force may result in accusations of sexual abuse or rape. This will lead to personal, familial, and even legal problems.
- And even when there is consent, especially from a recently known or a casual sexual partner, the wise teenager needs to be aware of the partner's covert purposes. Your partner may want to have sexual contact with you to punish another of his or her lovers; to use, take advantage of, or otherwise deceive or hurt you; to produce a pregnancy for dependency or financial reasons; to express covert hostility by infecting you with a venereal disease; or to "score" and then brag about it.

The therapist will be available to clarify any information the teenager obtains from any source in the context of a steady, mature and healthy sexual relationship -- mutual respect, trust, affectionate care, caution, and responsibility.

Wise adolescents will prefer to wait until they reach the age, maturity, and responsibility that gives them readiness for a meaningful steady, caring, and loving sexual relationship. Some teenagers will ignore these and other cautions as old fashioned sermons, become involved in diverse risky sexual activities, and experience any of the previously mentioned negative consequences. In their struggle to deal with such consequences, some teenagers may react with feelings of inadequacy, poor self-esteem, loneliness, sadness, and social isolation; some may develop increasing anxiety, depression, and even psychosis. Others may deviate into self abusive drug misuse, and still others may become involved in delinquent and criminal activities, either by themselves or as members of gangs and cults.

CHAPTER 10

Drug Misuse And Addiction

Parents hope they can protect their children from it. Teachers see their students affected by it. Families are devastated by it. Adolescents and even young children are often pressured to experiment with it. What is "it"? Alcohol and other addictive drugs.

Drug misuse and self abuse with addicting drugs are not new. People in every era, in every generation and in every country have turned to drugs to reduce pain and fatigue or to produce physical mental and interpersonal experiences which, otherwise, would not be available. What is new today is the greater availability of nicotine, alcohol and other addicting drugs and substances, their increasing use by adolescents and even children, the increasing pressure for their use, their increasing devastating effects on the users and their families, and their increasing problems posed to schools and communities.

Also new today is the spread of the misuse and self-abuse with hard-core addicting drugs from youngsters of slums to those of middle class and wealthy homes. For instance, many fresh-faced teenagers become intoxicated with alcohol, "pot" cocaine, or other mind-altering drug or substance every weekend, even while baby-sitting; many honor students are on the border of addiction after snorting a few lines of cocaine even on a dare; many suburban 12-year-olds poison their young lungs with a pack-a-day cigarette; and many private school sixth graders take similar risks with sniffing glue vapors.

How do young people develop a serious drug problem, but continue to deny it or to rationalize it away? Isn't the problem really blown out of proportion? Do many kids really use drugs?

According to 1996 figures compiled by the U. S. Department of Education, 4.6 million teens have a drinking problem, four per cent of high school seniors drink alcohol every day, and alcohol-related accidents are the leading cause of death among young people 15 to 24 years of age.

Eighteen percent of high school seniors are daily smokers and 11 per cent smoke 10 or more cigarettes per day and 70 per cent of all children try cigarettes, 40 percent of them before they have reached high school. More than a third of all high school students have had enough marijuana to become high.

As tolerance for the drug develops, the user requires increasingly larger amounts to obtain the same effect, which leads to physical and psychological dependency or addiction to the drug. Although many people associate dependency or addiction with hardcore drugs such as cocaine and heroin, you should be aware that such problems are also caused by certain sedatives, tranquilizers, and other prescribed medications, by nicotine and caffeine, and by certain over-the-counter compounds for the relief of the common cold or pain.

Reasons Why Youngsters Do Drugs

Why some kids use addictive drugs? There is a mixture of reasons, including:

- Curiosity, experimentation, tasting and testing with substances unacceptable by mainstream society.
- Peer pressure: most parents have no idea of the importance youngsters place on being accepted by their friends and the lengths to which they will go -including experimenting with drugs or a dare- to gain this acceptance.
- Lack of parental supervision, religious beliefs and social supports.
- Widespread and easy availability of addictive substances.
- Persuasive messages about the "fun" and "glamour" of smoking, drinking and other addicting behaviors portrayed by some printed and electronic media.
- The search for personal pleasure in an increasingly hedonistic-oriented society.
- Boredom and the inability to use free time constructively.

- The search for different perceptions which they believe can be obtained from mind-altering drugs.
- Rebellion against parents, teachers and other figures of authority.
- Impulsive, self-centered, gullible, and defiant traits.
- Deficient critical thinking and personal and social responsibilities.
- Denial of or escape from problems and rationalization of drug use.
- Money, sexual favors and other rewards obtained from using and selling drugs.

Symptoms Of Drug Use

How can you tell a youngster is using drugs?

Being alert to the early warning signs that signal your youngster is using nicotine, alcohol, and other addictive drugs requires a keen eye. It is sometimes hard to distinguish between normal changes and changes induced by drugs in adolescents and children. But changes that are extreme, repetitive and last more than four weeks may signal self-abusive drug misuse. Ask yourself the following questions:

- Has your adolescent or child become careless about his or her appearance and personal hygiene?
- Does your youngster show signs of fatigue, drowsiness, stumbling gait, redness and dullness of the eyes?
- Has his or her eating or sleeping patterns changed?
- Does he or she have a runny nose or respiratory troubles?
- Has your youngster's relationships with other family members deteriorated?
- Has your son or daughter dropped old friends?
- Is he or she no longer doing well in school -- grades slipping, attendance irregular, behavior problematic?
- Has your youngster lost interest in hobbies, sports and other favorite activities?

- Does he or she have chronic and extreme mood swings?
- Has your son or daughter developed chronic restlessness, hostility, argumentative and defiant attitude, anxiety, depression?
- Does he or she show impairment of visual, auditory, olfactory, and other perceptions?
- Is he or she expressing confused, irrational, or delusional thinking?
- Does your youngster have any drug paraphernalia in his possession that may signal drug use such as pipes, rolling papers, small medicine bottles, eye droppers, butane lighters, or publications on drugs?

Positive answers, even to a few of these questions can indicate use of alcohol or other addictive drugs. However, a word of caution. These signs may also signal other kinds of physical or mental problem. If you are in doubt, have your family physician and other pertinent professionals examine your son or daughter (See Chapter 13).

Once you accept the reality that your child is misusing addictive drugs, it is time to leave that armchair, hit the ground running, and decide to fight the problem. Your own home may be the battleground in the war against addictive drugs.

A crucial strategy is to know the enemy. Learn everything you can about drugs: their physiological effects, uses, patent and street names, and the often deadly consequences of dependence, toxicity, overdose and withdrawal *(see Appendix-C).*

Learn strategies you can use on a day-to-day basis to help your youngster, some of which are discussed below in the section of parental management. Seek medical and counselling therapies for your youngster, and parental and family guidance. Participate, even with the whole family, in recommended therapies geared to eliminate or at least alleviate corresponding problems.

Finally, living with and trying to help an adolescent or a child who has a drug problem is physically exhausting and emotionally draining. Take time to assess your own strengths and weaknesses. Know that the most important and effective weapons you need in your arsenal are love, determination, and a commitment to prevail over the powerful weapons of drug misuse and addiction.

"Before my son began experimenting with pot, I didn't realize drugs were such a problem. But now that he is receiving treatment I know what's going on. My son has to work hard to get around me," said one mother.

Parental Management

What can parents do? When your words fall on deaf ears and your son or daughter begins to experiment with drugs, don't deny the problem exists in an attempt to avoid the painful reality.

Refusing to accept the reality that your youngster is using addicting drugs is a deceiving device. It may keep you from facing the problem, it may keep the neighbors from talking about it, and it may keep you perceived as the "world's best parent." The bad news is that, every time you deny the reality of your youngster's drug misuse, you give him or her one less chance at a clean, drug-free, healthy life.

Turning a blind eye may reflect an obvious admission that you are powerless and have surrendered. Instead of seeking treatment and dealing with the situation in a straightforward way, you allow your son or daughter to continue to go downhill toward self- abusive drug dependency. This will result in devastating consequences to your youngster and to you and your family.

Consider the following questions:

- Do you lie to "protect" your son or daughter from exposure, such as calling school or work to say your youngster is "sick"?
- Do you take on responsibilities he or she has abandoned such as completing school work?

- Do you routinely pay for damage to property caused by your son or daughter while under the influence of alcohol and other drugs?
- Do you often give excuses for his or her drug related actions?

If the answer to one or two of these questions is "yes," you are not being objective, but if your answer to most of these questions is "yes," you have become co-dependent to your youngster's drug dependence. This means that you are devoting so much time and so much energy to your self-abusive drug-misuser youngster that you are actually becoming dependent on these care-giving activities. Your youngster's drug dependency and your co-dependency turns into an unhealthy cycle.

How can you end this cycle of your youngster being a drug dependent and you a drug-co-dependent?

You need to recognize that maintaining such a cycle is harmful to your youngster, to you, and to the rest of your family. It leads him or her into becoming self-abusive with drug misuse. It leads you into becoming convinced that you are a worthy parent because you are absorbed in covering up your youngster's drug misuse. Now, it is time to realize that it is healthier for your youngster, and you and your family to reverse the course of the cycle. This means that you need to eliminate your co-dependency and to help your son or daughter to stop his or her drug-dependency.

How do you do that?

- Deciding to reverse the cycle with strong determination, patience, and consistency.
- Recognizing that no matter how painful and difficult it is, you must reverse the cycle if you really care about your son or daughter.
- Eliminating your unhealthy dependency on covering up his or her drug-misuse and drug-related behavior.
- Showing understanding with empathy about his or her difficulty in stopping the drug misuse or dependency.

- Enforcing the rule no-more-drug use with clear punitive consequences if broken and clear rewards if complied with.
- Maintaining affectionate care of your troubled son or daughter no matter how faltering his or her efforts are to stop the drug.
- Seeking professional treatment for your youngster, including intensive outpatient or even inpatient treatment program.
- Seeking professional guidance, and even specialized treatment for relatives of drug misusers for you and your family.

When dealing with a drug-user youngsters, for most parents it is easier said than done to refuse giving them money or paying their bills, to bail them out of jail, to stop making excuses to relatives and neighbors for their drug-related actions, or to seek professional treatment, particularly away from home.

Typically, even parents who have provided a stable and nurturing environment berate themselves: "We were too permissive," "We were too strict," *"If* only we had done such and such a year ago."

But rather than engaging in this futile chest beating, parents need to be strong enough to act with such confidence, determination, and perseverance that their children know exactly where they stand within their home.

There's not much we can do as individuals about some electronic and printed media that exploits youngsters's immaturity by showing the "glamour" of smoking, drinking, and using other addicting substances. But we can pull up the drawbridge around our own home to protect our children.

Professional Evaluation

If despite the efforts from you, your family, others, and your youngster, he or she continues to have a drug problem, you should consult pertinent professionals as discussed in Chapter 13.

In particular, when dealing with adolescents or children who are misusing or having drug dependency, a comprehensive evaluation is required, since it is often associated with problems with family members and others, and with impaired performance in school, sports, work, and other activities. At times, it is also complicated with physical, sexual and mental abuse, theft, violence, and other delinquent and criminal acts. Often, self-abusive drug users may deny the drug problem, underestimate the amount of drugs used, lie, manipulate the examiner, or fear the consequences of recognizing the problem. Because of these unreliable attitudes, it is advisable to obtain information from and participation of parents and other relatives, and when deemed necessary, collaboration of teachers, probation officers, and other people involved with your child or adolescent.

The self-abusive drug misuse may precede or may follow other psychiatric conditions such as mood, anxiety, personality, psychotic, and organic brain disorders, which require pertinent assessment and treatment. In addition, the youngster may have concurrent physical conditions, related or not, to the used drugs. Therefore, the psychiatrist, alone or in collaboration with other physicians, orders and evaluates baseline and other laboratory tests. Among these are screening and confirmatory tests of urine and blood that detect alcohol and other drugs. The psychiatrist performs a mental status examination to identify impairments of mental and behavioral functions. And, alone or in collaboration with other physicians, the psychiatrist evaluates the physical and neurological systems of the patient. The specific mental and physical disorders caused by addicting drugs are discussed in Appendix-C.

Professional Treatment

Diverse medical and psychosocial therapies for drug-related disorders are provided in private offices, clinics, hospitals and other inpatient treatment programs. Inpatient treatment is indicated when the young drug misuser or dependent shows intoxication, withdrawal, suicidal or homicidal attempts, gestures or ideation, repetitive running away, and impairment of daily functioning at home, school and in the community, which require daily multidisciplinary evaluations and therapies in a supervised inpatient program. Medications and other medical treatment are prescribed to relieve drug cravings and other drug related symptoms and to treat concomitant physical disorders.

The treatment of tolerance, dependency and associated mental and behavioral disorders are treated with diverse therapies involving a mix of the following: individual medical dynamic psychotherapy including medications and other medical treatment, group therapy, and occupational art and other therapies for the youngster; family medical dynamic psychotherapy for the youngster together with his or her parents, siblings, and other close relatives. The treatment of drug problems in adolescents and children involves the dynamic medical psychotherapy discussed in Chapter 14. Supportive organizations for helping drug users and their families are also helpful.

During the therapy process, as during the diagnostic evaluation, collaboration and participation of the youngster's parents, siblings and other close relatives are crucial.

Prevention

What can you do to prevent use of addicting substances by your youngsters?

Don't wait to react when you discover, after the fact, that your teen or child has a drug problem. Instead go into the preventive mode, even though he or she has never given you cause for concern, be sure they understand clearly, and at a very early age, that use of any kind of addicting substances will simply not be tolerated.

First and foremost, set a positive example. If parents smoke, drink alcoholic beverages, use stimulants, tranquilizers, and other drugs regularly, they are poor role models. And they can hardly expect their teens or children to take them seriously when they warn them about the dangers of experimenting with drugs.

When you talk to your children about why they shouldn't drink or use drugs don't simply say, "Don't drink or be pressured into experimenting with drugs because you're not old enough."

Be specific. Explain the reasons: "I know it's easy for kids your age to think you can take risks and nothing bad will happen. And maybe you can the first few times. But the truth is that, without being aware of it, you can easily slide into an addiction that will ruin your life."

Be consistent. Make it clear that, according to your rules, a zero tolerance for alcohol and other drugs is in effect at all times and in all places. Discuss the consequences of breaking the rules and what the punishment will be. Enforce the rules, and follow through with the punishment when your youngsters break the rules. If you don't, they will rightly consider you weak and "wishy-washy" and you will not only lose their respect, but most likely the battle to keep them drug-free as well.

Be reasonable. Don't add new consequences that haven't been discussed before the no drug/alcohol rule was broken.

Avoid unrealistic threats such as, "you will not see your friends anymore." Instead, control your anger or disgust and focus on the problem, rules and penalties.

Provide healthy entertainment. Help your youngsters feel life can be exhilarating without nicotine, alcohol, and other addicting drugs by turning them onto positive activities that provide fun, and a sense of self-worth and achievement. Everyone needs something to give their lives meaning and purpose.

Know your youngsters's friends and their parents. Be sure they know that their friends are always welcome in your home. Make your house an inviting place where youngsters feel comfortable. The decibel level of their music may make you flinch, but the flip side is that you know where they are and what they are doing.

Join other parents. Work with them to present a united front on rules about curfew, drinking and unchaperoned parties. Also, keep tabs on your youngster's whereabouts. If he or she is at a "friend's house", make sure you know that friend and his parents. If you have valid reasons, confirm his or her whereabouts.

Maintain close family ties. The link between family breakdown and drug use has long been recognized. As family ties weaken or break, the importance of peers and their values become all-important. Some yield to the unconditional membership in antisocial gangs and cults.

Keep the lines of communication open. Webster defines communication as "the giving and receiving of information . . ." Most parents have no trouble "giving" their youngsters information in the form of lectures. But they're usually a little weak in "receiving" what their children tell them. Listen to your youngsters with respect and empathy and you may be surprised at what you will hear.

Do not hesitate to discuss the use of nicotine, alcohol, and other addicting drugs with your son or daughter. Some parents are in denial believing their youngster couldn't possibly be attracted to these addicting substances. Some don't talk about addicting drugs because their parents didn't talk with them about it, or because they use such substances too. Others hesitate because they simply don't know what to say.

Young people live for the moment and most give little thought to where they will be five days from now, much less five years. So, when you discuss the dangers of nicotine, alcohol and other addictive drugs with your youngsters, be sure to focus on their immediate and long term damaging effects: drugs can ruin teens' chances of going to college, being selected for athletic activities, being accepted by the military, or being hired for a job. Today, many employers and athletic authorities routinely test for drugs before hiring employees and athletes.

Don't wait until the drug problem advances. Many young people in treatment programs say that they had used nicotine, alcohol, and other addictive drugs for at least two years before their parents knew about it. So begin early and talk often about the dangers of substance use.

It is true that parents have the ultimate duty to protect their children and adolescents from abusing themselves with addictive drugs. But it is also true that many parents and other concerned individuals need all the help they can obtain in understanding the complexity of the drug problems and in sending an effective wake-up call that their youngsters will follow: namely, that the misuse of addictive drugs is a one-way street which most certainly causes addiction and serious and long lasting problems of physical, mental and social health, and even death.

CHAPTER 11

Self-Abusive Alcohol Misuse

When he was a toddler, John used to sip his dad's beer and his adoring family thought it was "cute." Later, he increasingly "tasted" his father's beers while watching TV and would have to aid his mother in putting his intoxicated father to bed. By the time he was in third grade, John acted as bartender at his parents' parties.

One Saturday, John's parents came home early and found their 11 year old son and three of his friends sprawled drunk in the living room, which was littered with empty containers of beer and wine.

When they consulted me a week later, they were still in shock and asking, "What did we do wrong?"

It was an unpalatable truth, but I helped them recognize that, among other misconceptions, they had subscribed to the "Don't do as I do, but do as I say" form of parenting. They had payed lip service to programs that stress the lethal dangers of alcohol on children and adolescents, but had done little to reinforce this message in their own home.

Unfortunately, the story of John and his family is not unusual.

In my twenty years of practice in adult, child, and adolescent psychiatry, I have seen many families wracked with problems stemming from some form of substance abuse. In many of these families, the parents themselves had begun drinking in their childhood. Usually, they had started it in their own homes or in those of their friends. Many had later combined alcohol with nicotine and other drugs.

Consider the following startling statistics on alcohol abuse in children and adolescents:

- Data from Sarvia & McClendon, *Ed 270702* in rural Wisconsin and Michigan showed "forty two percent of sixth graders used alcohol in 1984." Likewise, data from Howell, *Ed 284924* in Springfield, Massachusetts, public schools showed "ten percent began in the first grade and 32 percent in the fifth grade in 1987."

- The National Institute on Alcohol and Alcoholism reported to the U.S Congress in January, 1990:
  - ✔ alcohol is used by more Americans than any other drug including cigarettes and tobacco
  - ✔ 73.4 percent of persons aged 12 and over reported drinking alcohol in the past year
  - ✔ 36.2 percent of the same age group reported smoking cigarettes
- According to a national survey released in June, 1991:
  - ✔ at least half of the nation's junior and senior high school students drink alcoholic beverages and many "binge" drink to relieve stress and boredom
  - ✔ 10.6 million of the nation's 20.7 million students in grades seven drink alcohol
  - ✔ 8 million drink weekly, 5.4 million binge on occasion,
  - ✔ 454,000 binge on five or more drinks in a row at least once a week

In response to this survey, U.S. Surgeon General, Antonia Novello concluded that "adolescents drink deliberately to change the way they feel and we know that the use of alcohol to, in effect, self-medicate is the trap door to full-blown alcoholism." Dr. Novello faulted parents, schools and alcohol producers for "failing to adequately educate teens about the ill effects of alcohol."

I have had to counsel parents who overlooked, minimized, or denied that permissiveness may initiate alcohol dependence in their children. They were "shocked" to learn about serious intoxication in their youngsters.

But, what about parents who don't drink or do it in moderation, don't permit their children to drink, and also have children who abuse alcohol? I have been struck by the vulnerability of many children and adolescents in "getting hooked" on substance misuse.

Most of those children who drink initially had hated the taste and effects of alcohol, but what was supremely important to them was the approval of their friends. If they resisted the pressure to drink they were "squares," "nerds," or "jerks" and became group outcasts. But, if they joined the group in drinking they gained instant and unconditional acceptance--something not to be taken lightly when you are a teenager or even a preteen.

Parents often make the mistake of underestimating the powerful influence of peer pressure. Many, even older adolescents feel insecure and are easily lead by peers, some of whom try to compensate for their own weaknesses through arrogance, subversion, and dominance.

Reciprocally, a teenager may overvalue group belongingness and fear to appear "different." Take a closer look at the friends of your own son or daughter. Don't most of them probably look like clones of each other? If one of the most popular in the group decrees that everyone wears torn cutoffs and oversized shirts and undersized jeans and Nikes, it's a safe bet that will become your kid's uniform.

So also, with the misuse of alcohol and other drugs. Unless you're raising your youngsters in a vacuum, it's almost impossible to shield them from the message that comes through loud and clear every time they turn on the TV, go to the movies, read a magazine, or look at a billboard. The message? Alcohol is a glamorous symbol of maturity, the magic ingredient that can transform a dull party into a "happening," and a frog into a prince. If the leaders of the pack or teenage "gang" consider a party as "not cool" unless alcohol and/or other drugs are available, don't lend your permission and car to your child. If you do, be assured he or she is going to have a great deal of trouble resisting social pressure and temptation.

Enhance positive and powerful influences on your kids such as properly idealized celebrities in sports, physical fitness, TV., music, dance, movies, theater, literature, religion, and art. Attractive role models can still be seen with soft drinks in their hands in some sit corns on TV. Their message should be that you can celebrate a happy occasion without using alcohol as a social lubricant.

What can you do to make sure your child understands the potentially lethal effects of alcohol when it is misused? You can't do it the day you discover him or her passed out on the floor or you are called to the police station to be told your child has been booked for disorderly conduct or drunk driving.

How Parents Can Help to Avoid
Self-Abusive Alcohol Abuse

The following are some ways you can help your children put alcohol in its proper perspective:

- Don't allow young children to sample your drinks and make sure your alcoholic beverages are not accessible to them at any time.
- Don't brag about your risky drinking bravery. Boasts, such as "Boy, I really hung one on last night and still made it home without a scratch," send the message loudly and clearly that getting behind the wheel under the influence of alcohol is a "macho" or cool thing to do.
- Don't use alcohol as a solution for your problems. Lost your job? Having marital problems? You won't find a solution in the bottom of a bottle, but you will teach your kids that alcohol can be the quick fix that will help them avoid confronting their own problems.
- Don't hold an in-house "happy hour" seven days a week. Let your kids know that it is possible to be happy and upbeat and to celebrate special occasions without any kind of drug.
- Learn and teach your kids all about addicting substances. Support elimination of alcohol and other drugs to minors. Support corresponding programs with the involvement of school staff, sport coaches, local and national teenage idols and when indicated, with police and judges.
- Provide your youngsters with fun-filled activities within and outside the family and encourage them to invite their friends. Help them to find their music, dance, sports, and other talents. Encourage them to participate

in girl or boy scouts, student group exchanges, and in
other positively rewarding groups.

- Finally, participate with them in counseling if this
becomes necessary.

CHAPTER 12

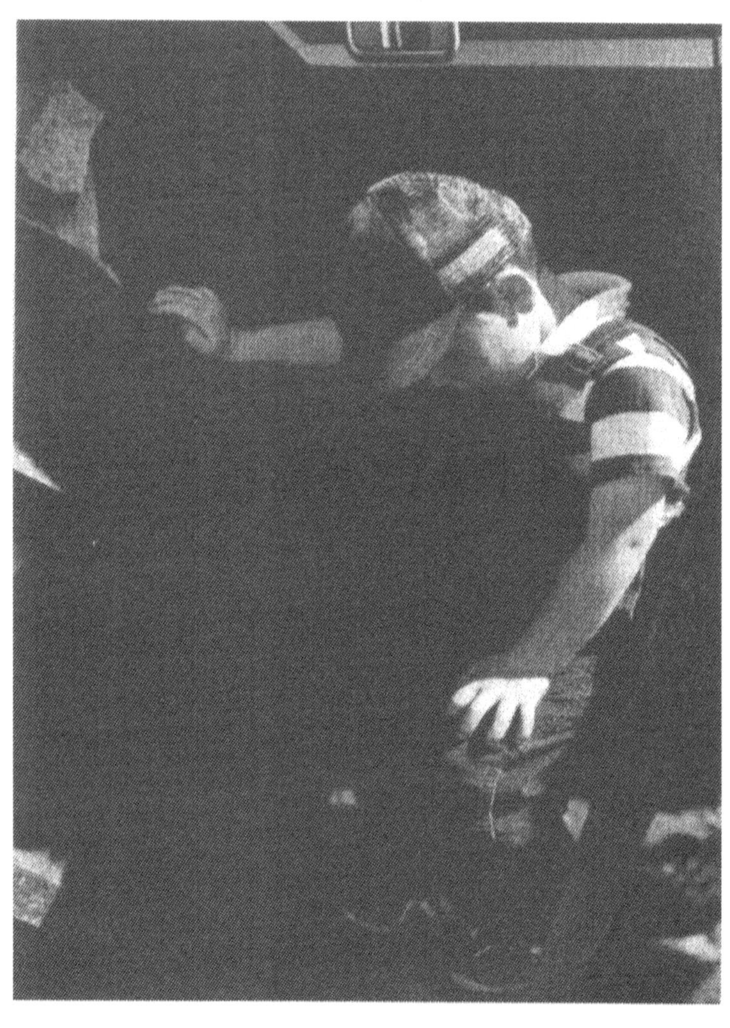

The mother of Kevin, a first grade grammar school boy consulted me. "I don't know what else to do for my son... his pediatrician finds nothing wrong with him. His doctor and his teacher advised me to consult with a psychiatrist" said Kevin's mother. She described Kevin as touchy, crabby, irritable, and demanding. He cried and whined too much and moved and screamed while asleep. He picked at his food and frequently complained of headaches, of feeling weak and fatigued. Kevin's pediatrician felt the boy was not gaining weight as he should.

Kevin's teacher described him as a good-hearted boy, but noted that he often complained of stomachache, headache, tiredness. She has observed that the other children in his class tend to pick on him and that he cannot concentrate, does not do assignments, and does not participate in other school activities. She finds him hesitant, doubtful, insecure, easily irritable, often stating, "I cannot do it, I am stupid."

Kevin agreed with all the above information. He commented that, "Nobody likes me, but I don't care, I don't care about anything."

Kevin is a child with a depressive mood disorder that began six months earlier after his parents filed for divorce and was exacerbated four months later after his father moved out of the home and his mother began to date another man.

Emotion, Affect, Mood, and Mood Disorders

There are differences in the concepts of emotion, affect and mood. *Emotion* is a complex feeling state with physical, mental and behavioral features and is related to affect and mood. *Affect* is the external expression of emotion observed by others and it may be in direct opposition to the person's own description of his or her emotion. *Mood* is the internal, sustained, and pervasive emotional state perceived through a sequence of feelings and attitudes about oneself, others, and the surrounding environment.

In the U.S.A., studies have reported the incidence of depression in children to be 0.9 percent in preschoolers, 1.90 percent in school age children, and 4.7 percent in adolescents. Mood disorders such as Major Depressive Episode, Dysthymic Disorder, and Bipolar Disorder can occur in all ages, sexes, social classes and cultures. Mood disturbances --especially depressive disorders--are the most common psychiatric disorders, particularly in females.

Normally, an individual has a broad range of emotions that can be brief and sporadic, or experienced as ongoing moods, without any interference with daily activities. Some people may even experience sporadic and transitory mood changes that cause minimal difficulties in functioning. By contrast, an individual may experience a mood disorder when he or she shows intense and prolonged mood deviations, loss of control, severe distress manifested through physical, mental and behavioral symptoms, and impaired interpersonal, social, and occupational functioning. These pervasive mood disturbances are often called *depressive* and *bipolar* disorders.

Current evidence identifies depressive and bipolar mood disorders as the same essential disorder regardless of the age of onset. Physiological studies report that these disorders can include neurochemical abnormalities such as decreased neurotransmitter (serotonin, norepinephrine, and dopamine) activity. There are also hormonal disturbances and sleep problems.

Mood disorders run in families. Studies have shown that incidence of mood disorders is higher in the children of mood disordered parents and in the relatives of mood disordered children. Nevertheless, no genetic association has been consistently replicated, although the risk increases with the number of family members who have a mood disorder. Many children raised by parents or surrogates with depression during their first two to three years of life, frequently develop depression later.

Freudian psychoanalytic theory alleges that a real or symbolic loss of a loved person is perceived as rejection that leads to depression, that mania and elation are a defense against underlying depression, and that the rigid superego punishes a person for guilt feelings about unconscious sexual or aggressive impulses. The internalized ambivalence causes pathologic mourning, and that this mourning takes the form of severe depression with feelings of guilt, worthlessness, and suicidal ideation.

No single personality trait or type has been established as being uniquely predisposing to depression. All humans at any age can become depressed. However, individuals with certain personality types (oral dependent, obsessive compulsive, and hysterical) may be at a greater risk for depression. Learned helplessness and misinterpretations of life experiences, negative self-evaluation, pessimism, and hopelessness are common in persons with depressive disorder.

Major Depressive Disorder

Major Depressive Disorder is manifested in children and adolescents with a mixture of the following symptoms:

- decreased or increased appetite, insomnia, hypersomnia or restless sleep, weight loss, slow movements or agitation, persistent fatigue or loss of energy, constipation, and other physical ailments without evidence of physical cause
- depressed mood, decreased interest or loss of pleasure in many activities, feelings of worthlessness or excessive and inappropriate guilt, decreased ability to concentrate and think, indecisiveness, suicidal thoughts, gestures, or attempts
- interpersonal difficulties, social isolation
- aches and pains

Dysthymic Disorder

Dysthymic Disorder is manifested in children and adolescents with a mixture of the following symptoms:
- fatigue, decreased concentration, thinking and memory
- depressed or irritable mood, poor self-esteem, decreased or loss of interest, hopelessness, feelings of guilt
- worries about past situations
- interpersonal problems, social isolation
- decreased ability to perform activities, impaired functioning

Bipolar Disorder

Bipolar Disorder or Manic Depressive Disorder is the most dramatic of the depressive or affective disorders. It is rare in prepuberal children. Adolescents with a bipolar disorder experience mood swings from depression to mania, usually with normal moods in between such two extremes. During the manic episode the adolescent shows the following symptoms:
- elated, expansive or irritable mood, grandiosity, grandiose delusions, rage, or paranoia
- hyperactivity, exaggerated planning, or participation in many activities, decreased sleep
- pressure to talk, racing thoughts, distractibility, disorganized and incoherent thought process
- reckless actions, interpersonal problems, impaired functionion

A person with a bipolar disorder may have normal mood and behavior after the manic episode, but eventually experiences a depressive episode with the same symptoms of the major depressive disorder mentioned above.

Mood disorders, both depressive and bipolar, need to be differentiated from other disorders, such as: grief; mood disorders due to medical conditions such as: Mixedema Madness (Hypothyroidism) and Madhatter's Syndrome or chronic mercury intoxication (poisoning) producing manic, and sometimes depressive symptoms; Schizophrenia; Substance induced Mood Disorder; Personality Disorders; Adjustment Disorder with Depressed Mood; and Schizoaffective Disorder.

A depressive or bipolar disorder may cause any of the following complications in a child or adolescent: disturbed physical health; impaired interactions with family, peers, teachers and others; poor performances in school, sports and other activities; reckless, delinquent or other antisocial actions; disbelief in or excessive concern with religion; escapist behaviors with self-abusing intake of alcohol and other drugs; membership in antisocial gangs and cults.

Serious and common complications of pervasive mood disorders are suicidal ideation, gestures or attempts, especially in those with a history of suicide in the family. Studies have reported that suicide in adolescents has increased significantly in the past several decades. Without treatment a depressive episode usually lasts from 10 to 12 months, and a manic one as long as three months.

If you are an adolescent or a child who is beginning to experience the symptoms of any mood disorder mentioned above, you may try to help yourself by doing the following:

Self-Help Strategies for Youngsters

- Do you understand that any mood disorder can occur in anybody regardless of age, that their causes may or may not be apparent, and that there is treatment available?
- Do you try to remember if your symptoms are related to certain events or circumstances?
- When did you begin to have depressed or elated symptoms?
- Did they appear following distress caused by your reaction to something that happened to you or to someone you care about?

- Are your symptoms maintained by your sustained distress related to any stressful condition experienced by you, your family, or others?
- Why are you feeling sad, lonely, depressed or elated, hyperactive, reckless, or manic?
- Why are you thinking so negatively about anything related to you, your family, others?

Usually, identifying at least some of the circumstances about which you are reacting with depressive or manic symptoms helps you to become less confused and more focused on what is distressing you. But to search for relief of your distress you need to change the way you are thinking, feeling, and behaving.

The journey from childhood to adolescence is full of pleasurable situations, but also full of obstacles and unpleasant events. Throughout this journey many experiences are similar and different for each person, regardless of their age. It is important for you to become aware of the pleasant and unpleasant experiences of your own journey--learn how to enjoy the pleasant circumstances and how to eliminate or at least decrease the stress of the obstacles encountered throughout your own path.

To increase your ability to handle the obstacles causing your depression or mania, follow your own journey's signs:

- Identify the pleasant and unpleasant experiences of your own path
- Accept yourself with both abilities and shortcomings
- Admit your mistakes, errors, misjudgments, and failures, and learn how not to repeat them
- Learn how to avoid as many new obstacles as possible
- Do not dwell on past negative experiences which cannot be erased
- Eliminate self-defeating, self-recriminating, and self-destructive attitudes
- Avoid using alcohol and other "mind-altering" substances--an elusive, escapist and self-abusive method

- Push yourself to interact with others in a meaningful manner if you become detached
- Push yourself to be active in athletics and other activities if you become inactive and isolated
- Push yourself to slow down if you become too active, to demanding on yourself, or too manic
- Remember, it is your own journey, so trust your capacity to make choices to go forward with confidence
- Decide what experiences you want in your life's path
- Accept and deal with the consequences of your choices and the events and situations that are not your choice and are out of your control
- Ask your parents, siblings, a relative, a religious representative, or another trusted person to help you

Parental Management

As concerned parents, you need to be aware of the symptoms of mood disorders in children and adolescents, so that you can observe such problems as early as possible in your youngster. You need to know if you or your own parents and other relatives have history of depression or mania, since these tend to run in families. If so, you need to know the names of medications that have been effective in controlling the depressive and manic symptoms of yourselves or your relatives, since such medications will have greater potential to control the similar symptoms of your youngster.

If you notice depressive and/or manic symptoms in your youngster,

- Show concern and empathy about his or her symptoms and related difficulties
- Ask him or her to tell you about any stressful situation causing distress
- Ask direct questions about possible problems with his or her physical health, school performance, or peers

- Explain that since you don't know what his or her problems are, you feel the responsibility to ask additional questions
- Explain that youngsters may not feel at ease in talking with parents about certain "private things"
- Ask directly if he or she is using alcohol, other drugs, or "mind-altering" substances, having sexual problems, is involved in some wrongdoing, or is having school, athletic, or other difficulties
- If your tactful, empathetic, straightforward, affectionate, and reassuring concerns are ineffective, then you need to consult a professional with experience in the evaluation and treatment of depressive and manic symptomatology in children and adolescents

Professional Treatment

As discussed in Chapters 13 and 14, diverse mental health professionals provide various methods to diagnose and treat depressive and bipolar disorders in children and adolescents. Child and adolescent psychiatrists assess the present and past history of depressive and bipolar symptoms in the youngster and his family members, the findings of diverse physical examinations and laboratory tests, the mental status of the youngster, the pertinent evaluations of other medical and nonmedical professionals such as teachers, formulates a clinical and psychodynamic diagnostic impression and designs an initial treatment plan.

In general, and according to personal preferences, psychiatrists treat depressive and bipolar mood disorders with any or a mix of the following therapies: medications to control the chemical and related imbalances, and to relieve impaired sleep, appetite, level of energy and other physical symptoms; individual, group, and family therapies, and parental guidance; relaxation, meditation, and biofeedback; and when indicated, referrals to other medical or nonmedical professionals, such as nutritionists, physical fitness trainers, and religious counselors.

Hospitalization is indicated when the youngster develops impaired functioning at home, school, or in the community, becomes self-abusive with alcohol and other addicting drugs, or becomes dangerous to himself or herself or to others.

Mood disorders in children and adolescents are common, run in families and may impair the functioning of the youngster in the present and in the future. At present, there is a general agreement that there is no evidence of a specific cause of depressive and manic disorders; that there are contributing factors such as biological, mental, familial, interpersonal, educational and other problems; and that there are medical and psychosocial treatments which are not completely curative, but are variously effective in controlling symptoms, providing relief of distress and improving impaired functioning.

CHAPTER 13

Professional Consultations

In this book I have emphasized ways to establish and enhance empathetic and affectionate relationships between parents and their children, so that when difficulties arise, most can be resolved within the family. However, if after a reasonable amount of time, these methods prove ineffective, professional counseling is recommended.

In general, diverse therapies are needed when the development of a child or an adolescent fails to advance or if it reverses to earlier stages. The following charts contain some disorders that call for professional consultation. As parents, you can use these charts to help yourself decide when to consult a professional to diagnose and treat the problem of your youngster and guide you toward increasing your ability to help him or her.

Infants

Physical
Retarded or regressive development of: eating and sleeping habits, eye movement, smile, visual, auditory and cuddling responses, reflexes (e.g. grasping), muscular tone and movements, speech (single and double vocalization, babbling single words and short sentences)

Emotional and Cognitive
Repetitive and intense anxiety, sadness, thumb sucking, crying, head banging

Interpersonal
Excessively detached, hostile, anxious or disturbed interactions with caregivers and others

Parenting
Rejecting, fearful, melancholic, punitive and other negative reactions of parents or surrogates toward the baby

<h1 align="center">Toddlers</h1>

<u>Physical</u>

Delayed or regressive development of: perceptions (visual, auditory, olfactory, tactile, gustatory), throwing a ball, walking, toilet training, object control, speech

<u>Emotional and Cognitive</u>

Intense anxiety about strangers and separation from parents and other meaningful persons, and excessive fears, phobias, compulsions, nightmares, sadness

<u>Interpersonal and Social</u>

Disturbed behaviors (as described for the infant) and recurrent aggressive behavior to self or others, excessive self-stimulation of genitals

<h1 align="center">Elementary School Age Children</h1>

<u>Physical</u>

Impaired development of sensory and motor functions and bodily growth; serious problems with appetite, sleep, energy, excessive masturbation

<u>Emotional and Cognitive</u>

Anxiety, depression, excessive distractibility, hyperactivity, and impulsivity, excessive nail-biting, impaired comprehension, fears, phobias, and compulsions, hallucinations, false ideas of being persecuted, poisoned, ill, abandoned

<u>Interpersonal and Social</u>

Serious conflicts with family, peers, teachers, coaches and others, school phobia or poor attendance, impaired study habits, conflictual sexual identity, excessive disrespect for rules, self-abusive with alcohol, smoking, nicotine and other drugs

Spiritual

Conflictual faith and fear of transcendental punishment associated with emotional, cognitive and behavioral disturbances

Puberty

Physical

Delayed or regressive development of body growth and functions

Emotional and Cognitive

Intense and conflictual worries -- in boys, about a sudden spurt or lack of skeletal or muscular growth, change of voice, facial hair or acne, sexual attraction to girls, spontaneous or provoked penile erections and ejaculation and in girls, about menstruation, vaginal discharge, breast development, sexual attraction to boys, masturbation. In boys and girls, conflictual reactions about erotic teasing or sexual advances at home, school and elsewhere, premature homo-or heterosexual crushes and rivalries, misconceptions as to allegedly devastating effects of sporadic self- or mutual masturbation, poor self-esteem, impaired self-identity, depressive, guilty, anxious, fearful and panicky reactions, exaggerated fears, phobias, compulsions, excessive distrust, suspiciousness or delusions of grandiosity or persecution or poisoning, impaired visual, auditory or tactile perceptions (hallucinations)

Interpersonal and Social

Poor relationships with family, peers, teachers and others, impaired learning, social isolation, legal problems

Spiritual

Fear of divine punishment or fear of satanic or other spirit possession or persecution

Early Adolescence

Physical

Disturbed bodily organs and functions

Emotional and Cognitive

Excessive mood changes, sadness, loneliness, anxiety, depression, obsessions, compulsions, hallucinations, delusions, poor self-esteem, impaired self-identity, self-abusive with alcohol and other addictive drugs

Interpersonal and Social

Conflictual relationships with family, peers, teachers and others, running away, underachievement, truancy, discipline and other school problems, vandalism, robbery, fire setting, promiscuity, delinquent, satanic and other criminal activities, reckless and unsafe sexual intercourse and its consequences such as unwanted pregnancy, abortion and sexually transmitted diseases (STD)

Spiritual

Extreme deviance from childhood faith, morality and life philosophies which clash with familial and societal traditions and causes emotional problems. For instance, deviance from Christianity or Judaism to cultism, mysticism, satanism, magical activities or disabling self-mortification

Middle and Late Adolescence

Physical

Repetitive complaints about body and its functions, (e.g. sexuality)

Emotional and Cognitive

Unsure and distressing male or female identity, excessive moodiness, poor self-esteem, and insecurity, anxious, depressive, obsessive and compulsive behaviors, hallucinations, and paranoid and other psychotic behaviors

Interpersonal and Social
Failures in achieving work and student roles, failures in performing the masculine or feminine roles assigned by society, intense resentments and distress about family and society, isolation, fanaticism, fire-setting, stealing, physical and sexuality problems, physical, sexual or mental abuse, individual and gang delinquency, vandalism, vagrancy, robbery, violence, homicide, satanic, and criminal cult activities

Spiritual
Extreme and conflictual deviance of faith, as discussed in "Early Adolescence" listing

Choosing a Therapist

As parents, you may choose a qualified professional, or if your youngster is facing legal charges, accept one designated by the court. However, if you feel that a consultant appointed by the court represents a form of extended police parole, you can ask permission to choose a professional advisor. In this case, ask your family physician, priest, minister, rabbi, family members, good friends, or other knowledgeable and trusted people to recommend a competent psychiatrist or other mental health professional.

Always check the qualifications and references of anyone you are considering to counsel your youngster and yourself. One way to do this is by asking about this person's qualifications from the staff of his or her corresponding mental health organization, hospital, clinic or other institution. Also look at the therapist's qualifications in the directories of medical and mental health care specialists available in most libraries. Do not hesitate to directly ask the therapist for information about his or her training, experience, and success in helping children, adolescents, and families. It is important that both you and your youngster and other family members feel comfortable with whomever you choose to go to and that the professional feel comfortable with all of you as well. This rapport is crucial for the development of mutual empathy and trust which enhances therapeutic success.

The psychiatrist, preferably one trained and experienced in helping children, adolescents and families will arrange the first interview according to preliminary information and other considerations he or she gathers from you, your son or daughter, relatives, and the referring person. Then, the initial interviews usually proceed as follows:

- If the patient is a child, usually, the psychiatrist interviews the child alone after having interviewed his or her parents together and separately, preferably on an earlier day. Then the therapist interviews the child together with both parents and then the child with each of them; if indicated, all family members are seen together during these initial sessions.

- If the patient is an adolescent, usually, the psychiatrist interviews him or her alone first to dispel suspicion and distrust and to establish initial rapport and trust. Then the consultant interviews the parents both together and separately to evaluate their concerns, interactions, and cooperation with the evaluation and therapy. Finally, the psychiatrist interviews the adolescent and his or her parents together to evaluate their verbal and nonverbal interactions, alliances or reciprocal resentments, and hostilities. When indicated, the psychiatrist interviews the adolescent together with all the family members to evaluate the family organization, interactions, alliances, rejections, scapegoat, support, and motivation to cooperate with the evaluation and therapy.

Whatever the choice for the initial sessions, the professional clearly states that all communications from the child, or adolescent, or any family member will be kept completely confidential, except when the disclosure indicates actions that would seriously endanger the youngster's or anyone else's life or welfare. The therapist will not assume the role of policeman, parole officer, judge or moral minister, but will be a friendly professional trained in understanding personal, familial, and other interpersonal and social difficulties and will help in resolving them in the best interests of all concerned.

The therapist will stress that future interviews would be only with the child or adolescent individually or in group -- although there could be sporadic meetings with the parents together or separately and or with family-members, but only after mutual agreement by all. However, sessions with parents and other significant persons should be more frequent when warranted by impending crises such as physical, mental, or sexual abuse, self-abuse with alcohol and other addicting drugs, and serious school and legal problems. Frequently, family therapy is recommended with participation of the youngster and his or her parents and siblings. When necessary, especially when culturally accepted, grandparents, aunts, uncles and other extended family members are included.

If the child or adolescent has severe mood swings, anxiety and/or is self-abusive, and especially when he or she has potential for homicide or suicide, hospitalization is necessary; this is explained to the youngster and his or her parents or surrogates. However, if the patient is dangerous to himself, herself, or others and if in spite of warnings, hospitalization is rejected, the therapist needs to ask the patient and his or her parents or custodians to sign a note refusing such recommendation and releasing the therapist from all clinical and legal liabilities, and to ask a witness to sign it. The therapist then needs to call the police and fill out a petition to hospitalize the patient involuntarily -- all of which is needed to protect the patient and others in contact with him or her.

In addition to psychiatrists, many mental health professionals such as clinical psychologists, mental health social workers, and specialized nurses provide individual, couple, group, and familial counselling. Family physicians employ laboratory tests, work with nursing and social and mental health agencies, and utilize modern modes of diagnosing and treating physical illnesses associated with many mental disorders.

As physicians, general psychiatrists combine these medical skills with at least three years of additional training and experience in analytic, behavioral, psychosocial, aesthetic, and other modes of intrapersonal and interpersonal treatment. Child and adolescent psychiatrists are general psychiatrists with at least two additional years of training in the diagnosing and treatment of biological, psychological, and social disorders of children, adolescents, and families. Many nonmedical mental health professionals and psychiatrists do mutual collaborative work in comprehensive therapy.

The first step in diagnostic evaluation and therapy is to obtain a history separately from the youngster and his or her parents, and, if necessary, from other relatives. Then the positive and negative influences of the youngster's biological, psychological, familial, educational, social, and cultural background must be evaluated.

The therapist obtains relevant facts wherein each informant recalls only what he or she wishes the therapist to know at the moment. There are, therefore, no inconsistencies in the various reports; rather, they indicate each informant's thoughts and prejudices, and how they might be altered as the interpersonal treatment progresses.

When indicated, a psychiatrist may, preferably in the presence of a parent of the child or adolescent and a nurse or other staff member, conduct a physical and neurological examination of the youngster, and, if warranted, refer him or her to a laboratory for urinalysis, blood count and chemistry, x-rays, thyroid profile, electroencephalogram, electrocardiogram and other tests. In the great majority of cases, the parents are thus assured that no evidences of a contributory illness have been found, and interpersonal therapy may proceed.

It is the therapist's job to persuade the youngster that far from being a violation of confidentiality, the family's cooperation in his or her treatment is not only essential, but would also diminish any feelings of alienation. However, in cases of physical or sexual abuse, or incest, the therapist is expected to conform to local laws which usually stipulate that such abuse must be reported to the proper authorities.

The therapist should join the child and parents in a therapeutic program contingent on the nature of the problems, the needs of all concerned, and the therapist's resources and versatility. Clinical psychologists employ tests such as Bender or Visual-Motor Gestalt, Neuropsychological, Ror-schach or projective, Minnesota MultiPhasic Personality Inventory or MMPI, Thematic Apperceptions or TAT, Stanford Binet, and Wechsler Intelligence Scale for Children or WISC and other tests to evaluate the child or adolescent. Then the psychologist may provide behavior modification, individual, couple, or group and family therapies.

Mental health social workers do psychosocial evaluations and also offer individual, couple, and group and family, and other therapies. Mental Health nurses do psychophysical evaluations and help the youngster regain physical health and also provide individual, couple, group, and family counselling. Religious counselors help the child or adolescent to regain a sense of spirituality. Teachers, coaches and other mentors may all play desirable supportive roles in helping a troubled youngster.

In general, many child and adolescent psychiatrists deal with the physical, mental, and sociocultural issues of human behavior, but especially deal with more serious deviations of conduct. They are trained to inquire more deeply and analytically into the causes of the problems. Many psychiatrists can provide balanced combinations of all of the therapeutic modalities outlined above, and in addition, can order and assess modern laboratory tests to diagnose physical disorders that can be associated with behavioral problems, and, because they are medical doctors, can prescribe medications and other medical treatments.

Parents should be informed of the rationale of the therapeutic procedures to be employed, their probable duration and costs, the frequency of the visits, occasional complications, and how best to cooperate with the therapist for optimal results. With the patient's signed consent, parents should be reassured that the therapist will initiate and welcome communications from them, teachers, and others concerned with the child's or adolescent's progress, and will arrange meetings whenever advisable.

Conversely, parents should be cautioned that they should not withdraw their child from treatment during an improvement or a temporary setback, since premature termination would seriously handicap later attempts at therapy.

It is important for parents to understand that therapy is an ongoing process, and that like many things in life, can have its ups and downs. The main consideration should always be what is best for the child or adolescent, and, in turn, for his or her family, and how the parents and therapist and youngster can work together to obtain the best result for all concerned.

CHAPTER 14

Dynamic Medical Psychotherapy

A therapist can interpret the thoughts, emotions, and motivations of others only through their behavior, since their words can be either a revealing or a misleading cue. Behavioral functions include the capacities for sensations, feelings, perceptions, memory, motivations, and adaptation -- how someone perceives himself or herself, others, and the environment.

At present, the comprehensive term "biopsychosocial" is the most inclusive and thus the most appropriate for the integration of concepts related to diagnosis and therapy of behavioral disorders. The term means that biological, psychological and social factors influence normal and deviant human behavior, and the diagnosis, treatment, and prevention of behavioral disorders.

The *biological* factors include heredity, physical health, and physical vulnerability and illnesses.

The *psychological* factors refer to the brain's ability to produce ideas, emotions, perception, memory, motivations, and awareness of one self, of others, and of the environment.

The *social* influences include the beliefs and customs from one's family, culture, and society.

There are similar biopsychosocial factors that determine human behavior, but the type and intensity differ in each person. These differences result from the different biological, psychosocial, and social experiences of each person. In addition, these factors influence each other.

For instance, a teenager who chooses to believe that his or her panicky (psychological, mental) reactions to a situation are due to witchcraft (cultural), may become isolated from others (social), develop stress-related gastritis (physical), or be afraid of divine punishment (spiritual).

I am writing about the dynamics involved in the process of dynamic medical psychotherapy because it might help in your understanding of and participation in the healing of behavioral problems. In dynamic medical psychotherapy, the psychiatrist does a comprehensive evaluation of the physical, psychological, cultural, and social factors related to the problem, as discussed in Chapter 13.

In brief, a psychiatrist or another physician does physical and neurological examinations and orders laboratory tests, to evaluate the patient's current physical status. These examinations are necessary to detect physical conditions that may be associated with behavioral problems; to evaluate the type of medications needed or to avoid; and to assess other medical or even surgical interventions that could be necessary.

A psychiatrist may prescribe medications to promote sleep, to eliminate headache or other pain, and to control depressive, anxious, violent, psychotic and other symptoms. A primary physician, a neurologist, or another medical or surgical specialist may treat corresponding physical ailments that are present in addition to behavioral problems.

Besides the medical methods of treatment, dynamic medical psychotherapy uses psychosocial methods to help eliminate or at least modify and relieve the distress caused by the problem. Usually, the distress results from actual, anticipated, or imagined physical ailments, interpersonal insecurities, and conflictual faith and other beliefs.

How you obtain healing from problems through dynamic medical psychotherapy depends on the following twelve crucial *healing dynamics:*

1. *Healing Hope* that you as an adolescent, child, and parent have in seeking help will increase your acceptance of therapy.
2. *Anticipated Confidence* that you have in the psychiatrist as trustworthy and competent will motivate you to participate in therapy.
3. *Rapport* or mutual trust and confidence of the therapeutic relationship between you and your psychiatrist will promote mutual participation and mutual success in therapy.

4. *Evaluation* of your current problems and the situations that precipitated them and contributed to them will help to focus on specific problems and ways to resolve them.

5. *Relief of Symptoms* through medications and other physical methods and through advice to eliminate or modify unhealthy feelings, thoughts, and actions will allow you to concentrate on and work through the dynamic psychosocial process.

6. *Insight* or your realistic understanding of your problems and their causes will help you to resolve them.

7. *Replacing Unhealthy Thoughts* that are contributing to your problems with healthy thinking will improve concepts you have about yourself, others, and your environment.

8. *Replacing Unhealthy Feelings* causing your distress with healthy feelings will improve the way you feel about yourself and those around you.

9. *Eliminating Unhealthy Communications* producing conflictual interactions with others and causing you distress will improve your ability to maintain healthy interpersonal relationships.

10. *Eliminating Unhealthy Actions* will improve your behavioral problems.

11. Replacing *Unhealthy Gratifications* from irrationally dependent, aggressive, revengeful, dictatorial, and escapist behaviors with healthy satisfactions from socially acceptable behaviors will be more rewarding to you.

12. *Using Improved Behavioral Patterns* in a progressive and ongoing manner will help you to resolve your problems and to improve your self awareness, your interpersonal relationships, and social adaptation.

Your understanding of and your active participation in the above twelve crucial healing dynamics will help you to resolve your problems.

It is important to understand that most sessions will be held with you and your psychiatrist seated facing each other; however, you may be asked to turn your seat or to recline in a couch. These positions relieve you and your therapist from constantly looking at each other. They promote your relaxation and your spontaneous verbal and nonverbal communications and prevent your constant inspection and possible misinterpretations of your therapist's movements and reactions. By promoting a therapeutic environment instead of a simply conversational one, the seating arrangement will enhance mutual objectivity in you and in your therapist.

To increase the effectiveness of dynamic medical psychotherapy, it is crucial to understand and comply with the following:

- As mutually agreed by you and your psychiatrist, all communications will be confidential; your psychiatrist may take notes for future reference; information will not be available to anybody unless you give your permission or unless there is a court order. To avoid misunderstandings and interfering advice from others, you should keep the issues of your therapy to yourself.
- Communications between you and your psychiatrist must be absolutely truthful. You need to express your feelings, thoughts, needs, desires, emotions, and fantasies in a spontaneous, open, and honest manner.
- Unless there is an actual reason to do so, the psychiatrist will not take your reactions toward him or her personally, but as reflections of your past or present feelings and attitudes toward other persons who are important to you.
- The therapist helps you realize that eventually others will hold you accountable for your actions; that your personal responsibility includes your actions resulting from careless use of alcohol and other substances; or from refusing to take medication to control your aggressiveness and other symptoms; or from other irresponsible attitudes.
- The therapist also helps you realize that what you do or do not do is your own decision; that your choice to do or not to do something may be favorable or unfavorable to you. To someone missing school because of a hangover,

the therapist would point out that that person's personal reasons for drinking are stronger than the need to attend school.

- The therapist clarifies that he or she cannot control or will not try to control the reasons you have to do or not to do something; that he or she can help you to understand and to give up your motivations which have caused your problems; and to consider and then start behaving in ways which are favorable to you and acceptable to others.

During therapy, you may develop *resistances,* particularly to the process of exploring, identifying, and eliminating long-standing and preferred ways of handling situations. You may exhibit such resistance by forgetting, arriving late, or canceling appointments without a valid reason. Some patients even request termination of treatment after a few sessions, alleging that the therapist has cured all their problems, while still behaving in ways that reflect a wish to resist therapeutic change.

Termination of Therapy

In general, you and your therapist may agree to end treatment, when you achieve a reasonable degree of:
- appropriate physical health ·
- socially acceptable behavior ·
- psychological tranquility
- spiritual serenity

You may need follow-up sessions or a return to therapy when you face new difficulties or a specific crisis.

CHAPTER 15

Adolescents and World Peace

"Every gun that is made, every warship launched, every rocket fired signifies, in the final sense, a theft from those who hunger and are not fed, those who are cold and are not clothed. This world in arms is not spending money alone. It is spending the sweat of its laborers, the genius of its scientists, the hopes of its children... This is not a way of life at all in any true sense. Under the cloud of threatening war, it is humanity hanging from a cross of iron."

-Dwight David Eisenhower (1986)

In the waning days of Word War II, Hitler's "Thousand Year Reich" lay in ruins. The vast majority of its weary and disillusioned troops were engaged in ferocious battles with the advancing Soviet armies on the Eastern Front. As a result, there were few troops to spare to the Western Front after initial German resistance to the Allied invasion in the West. The final stages of that futile resistance were almost entirely fought by German adolescents too young to have been drafted earlier in the war--some as young as thirteen.

Nevertheless, they fought so well in the Ardennes and in the final assault on Germany against the better equipped and trained American troops that the Supreme Allied Commander, Dwight Eisenhower, mused that perhaps there was something in the German national character that made them better soldiers than those from other nations.

Today, around the world, even very young adolescents are almost as likely to *be* soldiers as to play at being soldiers-and the world is no longer surprised. In Iran, twelve, thirteen, and fourteen year olds have been slaughtered in human waves along the border with Iraq. In Lebanon, young adolescents have carried submachine guns and grenades as they guard adult prisoners, and in South Africa, black teenagers have been at the forefront of the revolt against apartheid since the beginning of the Soweto riots.

Throughout much of history, societies have recruited adolescents in this role when cultures came into conflict. Conversely, young people participated in the anti-Vietnam war movement of the 1960s, and European adolescents have been among the strongest supporters of the "Green" political parties-- movements which attack nuclear power and weapons, emphasize environmental issues and urge universal disarmament--a far cry from the militarism previously encouraged by most western governments.

The problems that societies face today make it imperative that adolescents take on completely new responsibilities. Increasing numbers of countries possess or will possess nuclear weapons and the means to deliver them. Virtually any conflict has the potential to end in a nuclear war that would end life on this planet. Humanity can no longer afford the luxury of war-- whatever its size or duration. Adolescents must begin to contribute as much to peace as they have to war, and be protected from mankind's rush to Armageddon.

If society is to help change the role young people play in cross-cultural conflicts, we must first understand the dynamics of the extraordinary appeal the military has exerted on the adolescents of industrialized nations. Only then will we be able to devise strategies which will satisfy the same needs the military offers, but in ways which are productive rather than destructive.

Military training and service satisfy the basic needs of young men and women in ways implied in television commercials aimed at recruiting. One covert appeal entails a socially acceptable outlet for the aggression typically associated with adolescent defiance and rebellion.

On the other hand, military training also replaces the uncertain, halting, and often slow progress from childhood to adulthood with a short, highly structured training period after which the trainee is formally initiated into the "adult" society of the corps. Moreover, the actual training period itself is structured specifically to respond to several adolescent needs. The new recruit is ritualistically stripped of all aspects of his previous identity. He is then offered the chance to assume a new identity successfully by a rite of passage in "boot camp." Since all the recruits undergo essentially the same training, and the same hazing, they form a peer group which is encouraged to exclude those who have not experienced the same rituals.

The training emphasizes the virtues of hard work, discipline, and teamwork to appeal to natural adolescent idealism. Finally, the rigid sexual segregation of the training program plays upon typical, though often latent, reactive ascetic ideals. In the end, the military system produces a highly trained and motivated young man or woman who is motivated to destroy a designated "enemy."

It is important not to underestimate the effect of such experiences upon adolescent males and females. Virtually all Western countries have adopted such indoctrinations and it has served them well. But as powerful as this structure is, it cannot meet the more constructive needs of adolescents, such as the basic desires for a future of physical, social, and emotional security.

For the first time nuclear annihilation threatens every human being. Even those who might survive an initial exchange of nuclear weapons face the prospect of a nuclear winter so severe, so widespread, and lasting that biologists estimate that upwards of 500 million people would die of starvation. Perhaps the most upsetting aspect of this scenario is that areas of the world untouched by the direct affects of nuclear weapons themselves would have their populations decimated nonetheless.

But nuclear war also destroys even when it does not actually kill. Numerous studies have detailed the sociopsychological damage wrought upon those who live under the constant threat of annihilation. These effects are particularly severe in the case of adolescents, because most of them have not assumed the responsibilities or experienced the reward of adulthood. In particular, the failure to lessen or eliminate the danger posed by nuclear war causes adolescents to question the reliability of adult society and inhibits their emotional growth.

As a society, we face the very real danger that if we don't do something to enable adolescents to contribute as meaningfully to the process of peace as they have to that of war, we may find that we have produced an emotionally stunted generation, which bodes ill for cultural progress.

How then, can society exploit the unique needs of adolescents to resolve conflicts peacefully? The ideal situation would occur if all nations realized that no nation can gain by nuclear war, and that it is in the national interest of every state to find ways to reduce tensions and hostilities. Even if individual states fail to involve adolescents in the peace process, groups within societies--schools, political parties, philanthropic foundations, and religious groups--can do much on their own.

Essential steps in this process must be educational. Adolescents and children are not too young to understand the threat of nuclear war. They experience real concern about the consequences of nuclear power in all of its forms. Societies must instruct them concerning the real issues surrounding nuclear power just as it teaches them about sexuality, drugs, and crime.

To remain silent about their fears in today's warlike climate is immoral. Governments and concerned groups within societies must expand programs which encourage adolescents to experience first hand the diversity of different cultures. High schools and colleges should stress the teaching of foreign languages and customs. Programs which allow adolescents from different cultures to interact with each other must also be encouraged.

Officially accredited exchange programs for high school and college students are particularly useful, since adolescents who have the experience of actually living in a different culture for a prolonged period will develop an empathy and tolerance for that culture's unique approaches to life. In turn, this will make them less likely to fall prey to propaganda and more likely to work actively for peace. For those for whom we cannot arrange a prolonged stay in a foreign country, shorter tours may be provided. But the important point is that the scope of all such programs must be greatly expanded to more than just the children of the affluent.

Finally, society must help adolescents temper their counterproductive defensive illusions that they are omniscient, that the rest of the world is as cooperative as their parents, and that they, therefore, can easily establish order and predictability in a world of chaos. It is society's responsibility to dispel such illusions which .can propel adolescents into dangerous political and cultist organizations.

As one way of breaking the motivational hold which military organizations have on adolescents, concerned groups in societies which have universal conscription should press for alternate forms of national service. Such service should aim at alleviating social problems such as poverty, illness, hunger, poor housing, and illiteracy. Thus, the adolescents who take part will see that the work they do is important to the society, and that such a program fulfills many of the same needs that military training presently meets, but to promote peace rather than violence.

In societies without conscription, concerned groups should make certain that alternative programs have greater prestige than the military. These programs must be advertised and be accorded honors commensurate with those of military service. Only in this way can we begin to wean adolescents, and eventually the society as a whole, away from the use of force in international disputes.

Unless concerned groups and individuals take steps such as those above to educate adolescents about the dangers of nuclear war, and ultimately war in general, and work to offer them ways to contribute peacefully to society, adolescents will continue to contribute to their *societies* in the only ways they are allowed or forced to. It is time we offered them a future better than that offered to previous generations. It is time to remove *adolescence* from the machinery of war.

Ways to Integrate Youngsters into the Search for Peace

- Educate children and adolescents to warn them of the dangers of nuclear power and nuclear war.
- Increase opportunities for adolescents to live in foreign countries and meet adolescents from other cultures.
- Renew emphasis on the teaching of foreign languages at all levels of schooling.
- Establish alternate types of national service for adolescents which use their talents for peaceful purposes.

APPENDIX-A

Why Children Behave as They Do

An adolescent boy is picked up by the police for breaking into a garage and stealing a bicycle. He stands apart defiantly as his father rants about having to take a strap to him more often, his mother cries, and his grandmother tells everyone who will listen that she knew he had a devil's heart. His school teacher says that she gave up on him long ago, and neighbors just shake their heads, talking among themselves about the mischief he had been in over the years. What has caused this boy to break the rules of society --his relationships with his parents, family, and community, or an emotional or other personal problems causing his deviant behavior? Can his parents and others around him help him or is he already lost?

It should come as no surprise that a healthy conception, pregnancy, birth and infancy of a child, and parents who care for each other and their offspring combine to make good relationships and a strong bond between parents and their children and teenagers. In turn, these influences contribute to a youngster's ability to enjoy future interactions with his or her parents, relatives, friends and others, and to enjoy a socially accepted adaptation.

Other influences such as genetic traits, physical and psychological health, social standing, religious, or folklore beliefs of the mother and father as well as other cultural influences also shape the behavioral development of children and adolescents. An obvious example the role society has on shaping behavior can be seen in some cultural beliefs that the left hand is "unclean." In this environment, if a child is born left-handed or suffers an accident to the right hand, the way that child perceives his or her own personal worth will be affected, and the resulting poor self-esteem may cause behavioral problems.

The degree and intensity of normal and deviant behaviors differ from one child to the next, since each has a different genetic structure and different cultural, psychological, and sociocultural needs and stresses. When such diversity of individual characteristics is considered, one sees how crucial it is to understand the behavior of each youngster, each parent, and their interactions with each other and with society.

Let me examine briefly each stage of a child's life through adolescence in order to better understand socially accepted and deviated behaviors that are discussed throughout this book.

Prenatal Development: The Bedrock of Human Existence

A woman's ovum (egg) and a man's sperm are single sex cells with 23 chromosomes apiece. Once a month, one of her ovaries releases one ovum, which is eventually discharged during menstruation. If the ovum unites in the Fallopian tube with one of the millions of sperms released during his ejaculation, a zygote, or fertilized human egg, with a full set of 46 chromosomes, is produced.

Males have XY chromosomes and females have XX chromosomes, which are split apart in the sperm and ovum, respectively. If the Y chromosome from the male unites with a female X chromosome, the resulting zygote will develop as a male-- XY. However, if the X chromosome of the sperm unites with a X chromosome of the ovum, the resulting zygote will develop as a female -- XX.

During the three months following conception, the fertilized zygote grows into an embryo, with a recognizable head, moving limbs, blood-producing liver, beating heart, nervous system, and a brain. All embryos are somatically "female" until about the sixth week of development, when embryos with XY chromosomes begin releasing the androgen hormone, which continues through the end of the third month. If this hormone is not released, then, the XY embryo will be a genetic male with female genitalia. During the final six months of pregnancy, the embryo develops into a fetus, with its organs becoming increasingly developed in form and function.

Balanced nutrition, physical fitness, and ongoing medical care of the expectant mother increase the possibility of a healthy conception, pregnancy, and childbirth. Conversely, chromosomal and other genetic defects, poor nutrition, self-abusive alcohol and other drug misuse, and other serious disorders of either parent can produce a pregnancy that may end in a miscarriage, a dead zygote, embryo or fetus, or a child born with physical defects.

To increase the possibility of a mother and father having a healthy child is to carefully plan its conception, including medical and even genetic consultations. If one or both parents have emotional or mental problems that impair their ability to raise a healthy child, then a psychiatric consultation is advisable. Prospective parents who cope well with daily stresses and who care for each other have a greater possibility of a healthy pregnancy.

In the absence of any physical problems, breathing and muscular relaxation exercises, such as Lamaze techniques for the expecting woman, and medical and other guidance for the prospective parents will enrich the experience of childbirth. This often helps in promoting a "natural" childbirth, which minimizes the distress of delivery. Even taking into account individual, familial and sociocultural differences, development proceeds in a rather similar manner for most children and adolescents.

Infants

<u>Physical Characteristics</u>

Newborns have puffy faces and eyes, wrinkled skin with fine hair and an oily covering called *lanugo,* that protected the fetus and helped it pass through the birth canal. Compared to adults, a newborn's head is misshapen and large in relation to the rest of his or her body.

Immediately after birth, newborns begin to breathe and cry spontaneously or with the help of gentle manipulation of the chest and arms. The puffiness, the soft fine hair, and the oily covering of the skin disappear during the first few weeks after birth. Often, two or three days after birth, the babies' skin becomes yellowish, a normal metabolic effect of a substance called *bilirubin*. This condition usually disappears in a few days; if not, medical treatment is advised. One of the reasons why pediatricians recommend that newborns and their mothers remain in the hospital at least 48 hours after delivery is to manage this and other problems that become apparent in the first few days of life.

Activity

Infants soon begin to respond to stimuli. When their palms are gently pressed, their small fist closes on the touching finger as though grabbing security. When their cheeks are touched, their lips move and their head turns toward the touched side as though seeking for the breast or bottle. When any of these is provided, their sucking skill is stimulated. When startled, their arms reach out (the "Moro" reflex), as though seeking embracing reassurance from other humans.

Several days after birth, infants turn to follow near objects with their eyes, and begin to recognize caregivers, especially the mother, by sight, sound, and apparently by odor, which is the most primitive of the senses. Even blind infants learn to reach and grasp by hearing sound cues or feeling air currents and vibrations. Taste, closely related to smell, leads infants to sucking longer on sweet liquids -- a preference that should not be repeatedly indulged to prevent obesity and other nutritional problems later in life.

Behavioral Patterns

These differ greatly among babies. And accordingly, they are described as *quiet, calm, sensitive, hyperactive,* and *resistant.*

Most mothers will describe their children as having any of these and other traits from "the moment they were born," which is truly no maternal exaggeration. As documented by long-term research studies, *temperaments* are mostly set genetically, although modified by intrauterine and later experiences.

Soon after birth, happiness is expressed by infants through smiling, gurgling, relaxing, or reaching. Tiredness, discomfort, and annoyance are shown through irritability and avoidance of stimuli. Anger and self-protection are apparent through muscular tensions and resistance. Hunger, physical distress, and pain are voiced through different cries, which are quickly recognized by perceptive parents and other sensitive caregivers. Infants are continually developing sensory, motor, perceptual, linguistic and intellectual capabilities.

Language

At about two months, infants repeat vowels, such as "aaaaah" or "ooooh." At about three months, begin to distinguish consonants, like "d" in daddy, "p" in papa, and "m" in mama and mommy. Around four to five months, a baby can repeat words, such as "mama," "dada" and "kaka." This babbling is practice for learning language, although fond parents often believe their infant is speaking real words and understanding the meaning.

At close to ten months, infants can form multi-syllabic words. At about one year, they begin to express associative meanings and intentions, such as "up," "again," "more," "bye-bye,' and "want."

At about eighteen months, most children begin to fully communicate, using sentences rather than individual words. Further linguistic development varies according to their personal abilities and experience. Physical maturation keeps pace with individual and sociocultural differences, but, at this age, it is usually more rapid in girls than in boys.

The Nervous System

There is brain "growth-spurt" in newborns which begins in the last prenatal trimester; however, the baby's lower (basal) areas, which control the physical roots of emotion, develop before the higher (cerebral) areas, which control the physical roots of cognition and creativity. It is important for all parents and others concerned to understand that the skills for receiving, storing, integrating, and utilizing knowledge begins in the newborn stage.

Awareness and Interpersonal Communications

At first, newborns cannot discriminate between themselves and their caregivers, who are perceived only as gratifiers of needs. As their development becomes more sophisticated, infants can identify their mother's face and breast. Soon also, they begin to distinguish internal from external stimuli, and become aware of their existence as separate from others, and thus begin laying the foundation of interpersonal relationships. Infants sense the presence and absence of others as reflected in the game of "peek-a-boo."

At about three to six months of age, they smile when receiving food, love and warmth. Around one year of age, they are able to maintain relationships and to express discomfort and insecurity in unfamiliar circumstances, which is known as *stranger anxiety*.

During the first year of life, most infants demand immediate gratification of their needs. As they become older, they develop a tolerance for delayed satisfaction. At around eighteen months old, most distinguish the shapes of objects and compare their size while perceiving color, odor, texture, taste, and sound. Parents become aware of these increasing abilities as their child, who once ate everything offered, refuses certain food because of its look, smell, taste, or even texture.

Optimum Care

Newborns are exceedingly sensitive and fragile beings who require intensive and affectionate attention to satisfy their needs. This includes such things as comfortable and warm clothes to stabilize body temperature; scheduled day and night breast or formula feedings; and hygienic disposal of excreta and urine. Just as essential to infants are concern, tenderness, solicitude and care provided by parents or guardians which serve as the foundation for reciprocal love and devotion with the family, and later on, with friends, lovers and others throughout life.

Toddlers

Between fifteen and thirty months of age, children further develop their abilities to talk, walk, feed themselves, and become toilet-trained. Thus, they become progressively autonomous and explicit in expressing their needs for physical, interpersonal, and affectionate care.

Physical Characteristics
Toddlers begin to lose their baby fat and rapidly develop muscles and bones. At around eighteen months, they develop more precise motor skills and can walk, make marks on paper (and sometimes walls and tables) with pencils and crayons, put together simple puzzles of two to four pieces, and snap pop-beads. They can even squat, though they still may fall over. As their development progresses, they can throw a ball, run, and climb stairs if one hand is held by someone. At around two years old, children can climb up and down stairs alone, run well, kick a large ball, and manipulate objects with their fingers and hands more efficiently.

Excretion and Toilet Training
At about eighteen months, most boys can control their urine and bowel movements, while most girls "toilet train" a little earlier. Initially, some toddlers may react to this novel experience by repetitively postponing and releasing excreta, and by playing with it or by examining, smelling, and even eating it. Thinking that it is a part of their body, they may not understand when they are disciplined or harshly punished for such activities, or may become upset when their excreta is thrown away.

Parents should gently teach the use of the potty or toilet only when the child is ready to do so, and at the child's pace. They should praise success, but avoid criticism or bribery. Coercion may cause frustration, anger, and nightmares, along with covert rebellion such as wetting and soiling of clothing and bedsheets. This reactive and conflictual behavior can later resurface in preadolescents and teenagers as shame, self-doubt, obsessive cleanliness, or other related disorders. Later, as adults, they may harbor resentments, or practice compulsive rituals, anal erotism, and reciprocal oppression of their own children.

Sexual Development and Masturbation

At around the age of two and a half years, toddlers begin to assume the attitudes and roles of boys or girls. This awareness comes from genetic, hormonal, parental, and other interpersonal influences and sociocultural factors. Boys may play with building blocks, wheeled toy devices, and windup mechanisms, while girls may enjoy soft toys, dolls, model houses, and dress-up clothes. Such preferences are highly predetermined by society as being of masculine and feminine interest, respectively. However, boys still join girls and girls play with boys with only slight differentiation of gender roles. Often this is expressed in exhibitionistic, exploratory, and comparative activities as they try to learn about their physical differences. Such behaviors are considered a normal phase of healthy development that pass with parental explanations and guidance, and need not distress parents and other persons.

As part of this physical discovery process and of physiological factors, boys may variously rub their penises and girls their clitorises for pleasurable sensations when tense, anxious, bored, tired, or sleepy. Toddlers may be diverted from this practice by parental attention and other distractions. Nevertheless, normal increasing erotism will frequently be exhibited later, especially during adolescence, and often by masturbation. Most professionals consider this behavior as deviant only when it becomes too much a part of a youngster's life.

Language, Intelligence, and Communications

Language skills leap forward during the toddler years when most children can combine two to three words in a "telegraphic" style; understand pronouns, many modifiers, compound sentences, sizes of objects (as in "so *big"*), and the meaning of their family hierarchy; most understand physical functions such as sleeping, eating, and walking, and use words to obtain attention and express their likes and dislikes.

Most toddlers will take turns in a conversation, but still cannot understand many words used by adults. This is why, when parents and caretakers speak to young children, they simplify their vocabulary and the speed of their speech, often repeating phrases and defining words with visual examples. If acquisition of language proficiency is overstressed by parents and others, toddlers can become resentful and stubborn. Like other learned skills, mastery of language develops when the child is ready and at a pace that is comfortable and unique for each child.

Research studies report that reading to toddlers and preschool age children increases their linguistic and cognitive skills.

Emotional Development

Emotions begin to play a part in toddlers' perception of people and environment around them. They express feelings of happiness, sadness, anxiety, and anger. They may exhibit fears of isolation, animals, strangers, the dark, and even storybook or television characters such as witches, monsters, and ghosts. These feelings often are exaggerated by apprehensions of parental separation and abandonment. Such anxieties increase young children's expressions of dependency and affection, which in turn, evoke specific reassurances through the comforting words and actions of their parents and others. Children's fears should be taken seriously and dealt with in a way that reaffirms their need for safety and love. Empathetic and affectionate handling of the toddler's feelings promotes a healthy emotional development.

<u>**Social Development**</u>

At around two years old, most toddlers can play alone or near others. This is known as *parallel play.* Some may show distress when pressed to play and share especially with other children. However, parents and other caregivers can help them learn to share, collaborate, give, receive, and other socially determined behavior. They can promote such learning by taking toddlers as frequently as possible into favorably stimulating places, such as a playground, where they can learn to imitate other children's appropriate interpersonal interactions. This will ultimately help them to resolve or decrease excessive self-centered conduct. Toddlers can be progressively taught skills of mutual sharing, helpfulness and caring, and concepts of morality, spirituality, and personal and social responsibilities. As they grow older, they can be enrolled in neighborhood primary or head start schools, where, with parental encouragement, they can learn to relate to children and adults of different ethnicity and cultures. Such interpersonal experiences help toddlers to develop healthy social skills.

If misunderstood, neglected, pushed beyond their individual capabilities, criticized, or harshly punished for their failures, toddlers, like adults, will react with rebellion, revenge, escapism, anxiety, depression, and other deviations of behavior that may require diverse therapies.

Preschool Age Children

Between the ages of two and a half years of age and six, children continue to need physical activity, family security, and a sense of personal significance based on their unique potential. This should be provided by their parents, educators, and others in their social environment.

<u>**Physical Development**</u>

Around the age of three, most children reach about half of their adult height and are thinner than most toddlers. Their physical abilities improve. Most can ride a tricycle, jump well, and alternate feet going up stairs. Between five and six, most can skip with alternate feet, coordinate arm, hand, and finger movements, manipulate complex toys, and even ride a two-wheel bike.

Gender Identity and Sexuality

Around the age of two and a half, male and female awareness has now become more clearly recognized and assured. Most boys between ages four and six have penile erections and most girls around the same age have clitoral erectile sensitivity, which provide pleasurable sensations and can increase the masturbation and mutual sexual exploration of the toddler's years.

Cognition

The thinking of preschoolers is full of curiosity and imagination. They make rapid conclusions, ask for explanations, and usually connect everything with themselves. Their thinking is constricted to immediate space and time and is limited in foresight, which is evident in their simple drawings, sparse writing, and ambiguous speech.

For most preschoolers, it is sometimes difficult to differentiate between the pretend and real. They may even regard dreams as actual awakened experiences. Parents can easily be frustrated if they do not understand that their three or four year old really does not understand these distinctions.

Information, Education, and Socialization

Even within their homes, children are currently subjected to constant bombardment by auditory and visual images, and messages conveyed by radio, television, video cassettes, the Internet, and other computer programs mostly intended for adults. While many of these influences are motivationally and intellectually beneficial, some may stimulate premature interest in violence, sexuality, and pornography.

Some may also glorify dishonesty, while emphasizing brutality and even mass slaughter.

It is imperative for conscientious parents, teachers, and government officials to monitor and counteract such misleading messages. Children must be protected by society, especially those who are deprived and neglected by their primary caretakers and who may be later easily seduced into sexual promiscuity, delinquency, and criminality.

About one third of all three year olds and most five year olds attend nurseries, day care centers, or Head Start classes where they receive instructions in speech, drawing, writing, and creativity. They also learn autonomous decision making, responsible interpersonal relationships, cultural diversity, personal and social responsibilities, and other introductory social skills. Playing with sand, water, dough, and story books, and even pretending, are not just games, but helpful learning devices for preschool children, which prepare them for their approaching primary school years.

Primary School Age Children

In classical psychoanalysis, the interval between assumption of gender identity and puberty was termed the "latency period." This is now largely considered a misleading concept, since during this time the children's physical, intellectual, affective, educational, and social experiences are abundant, not latent, and profoundly influence the development of their personality.

<u>Physical Growth and Skills</u>

Although primary school age children's rate of growth and abilities differ depending on individually unique genetic backgrounds and experiences, competent guidance helps children progress in their play activities, bicycle riding, individual and team athletics, and in the development of musical, artistic and other creative talents.

<u>Cognition</u>

At about six years of age, most children speak the language of their parents; at around nine, most delight in riddles, puns, jokes and attempts at sarcasm; by twelve, most are adept at ambiguity and conceptual absurdities. Slowness in these areas requires special attention by parents and teachers. The inability to understand simple stories or instructions, to describe recent events, or to speak in full sentences may indicate a linguistic retardation.

Seriously impaired reading, called *dyslexia,* is more common in boys than in girls. It may be due to combinations of genetics, trauma, or other problems. Often, there are related impairments of attention, memory and special orientation. Likewise, children may show deficient ability to write. Parents and other caregivers and teachers can help children learn to speak, read, and write, avoiding bribery, criticism, and punishment. Often, additional professional tutoring is required for these problems. If this guidance is not enough, special medical, educational, and psychological counseling should be obtained to improve such skills and prevent possible reactive emotional and behavioral problems.

Youngsters who show expanding capabilities for memorizing and categorizing data, discerning relationships, .and recognizing perception of space, time, and their significance, indicate their ability to acquire and utilize knowledge. This may signal special talents and even creative genius. These unusually high skills also require special attention by parents and educators. A child with unique talents may challenge parents differently. Mozart's father gloried in Amadeus' musical genius; the elder Johannes Strauss forbid his talented son to practice piano.

During primary school age period, children begin to experiment with slang and peer group fads, testing their language flexibility and the development of social contacts beyond parental influences.

Sexuality

There is nothing latent about the development of sexuality in primary school age children. This is also the time when children show interests in erotic publications, music, dancing, voyeurism, and homo-or heterosexual explorations, usually short of genital contact. Prepuberal boys may show concern about the size of their penis and its spontaneous or provoked erections. Prepuberal girls may express concern about their clitoral sensations and may wear padded bras prior to breast development and menstrual pads before menses begin. Empathetic guidance from family and teachers helps the development of these sexual interests and actions become a healthy sexuality. Conversely, excessive teasing, condemnation, and punishment for such behaviors of natural sexuality may seriously impair children's future sexual adaptations and may cause reactive emotional and behavioral problems.

Emotional Development

Around six years of age, most children become more able to experience, differentiate, and describe their feelings. They can recognize other people's emotions, they can compare themselves and their actions with others, and they can judge more specifically the appropriateness and inappropriateness of their own behavior.

APPENDIX-B

Why Adolescents Behave as They Do

Adolescence is a period of life initiated by rapid physiological, physical, and sexual growth accompanied by increased emotional, intellectual, social, and spiritual development. As with all other age groups, these factors are influenced by individual differences arising from genetics, interpersonal relationships, emotional and cognitive factors, and by customs, laws, rules, and language patterns the youngster has learned. Socially assigned roles differ among societies. Despite such individual, psychosocial, and cultural diversity, development is similar among most adolescents.

Physical Maturation

In boys, anywhere from age nine to fourteen, the hormone testosterone, which produces masculinization, deepens the voice, accelerates physical growth and muscular mass, increases facial, axillary, and pubic hair, enlarges the penis, intensifies erotic drives, and facilitates the ejaculation of active spermatozoids with reproductive capacity.

In girls, anywhere from age eight to twelve, the hormone estradiol, which produces feminization, enlarges the breasts and hips, advances the functions of the ovaries, vagina and womb, produces the first and subsequent menses and expels an active monthly ovum with reproductive capacity.

Testosterone and estradiol also influence the central nervous system activity, including mood and behavior. Increased testosterone has been associated with aggressiveness and impulsivity in some males, whereas decreased estrogen may cause depressed moods prior to menstruation in some females.

In well-nourished Western societies, physiological and physical development for both boys and girls starts earlier than in other parts of the world. Current studies report that in the U.S.A., many eight and nine year old girls are menstruating and developing pubic hair, breasts, and roundness of the hips--and that many are sexually active. In Western societies, early adolescence is considered to last from age ten to twelve for girls and from age twelve to fifteen for boys; middle adolescence from age twelve to fifteen for girls and fifteen to seventeen for boys; and late adolescence from age fifteen to eighteen for girls and age seventeen to twenty for boys. Some researchers claim that adolescence may extend even through the mid-twenties in some individuals.

Physical Characteristics

Because their physiological and physical features are changing so rapidly, and because of socially assigned roles, many adolescents are concerned and often preoccupied about their body and its various functions. Their physical appearance, strength, size, skills and increased sexual drives become a priority to them.

Preteen and teenage concepts and feelings about physical health may range from healthy aspirations regarding physical shape and fitness to preoccupations and irrational ideas about their bodies. For instance, some adolescents may turn normal body aspirations into obsessive preoccupation with physical appearance and performance, which can lead to self-abusive activities. Usually such behavior is rationalized as productive, and thus, they see their use of stimulants, tranquilizers, alcohol, nicotine, and other addictive drugs as arousers of the mind's "creativity"; they describe their exhibitionism as a "sexual catalyst"; they label their strenuous muscular exercise, irrational athletic performance, and even life threatening weight-reducing diets as "healthy" physical fitness; and they justify their sexual promiscuity as "a need for togetherness," "a signal of connectedness," and "making love."

Psychological Characteristics

Most adolescents, especially young ones, often experience a combination of polarities and ambivalent feelings such as: affection versus hostility toward parents, relatives, peers and others; respect and disrespect of authority figures; mixed feelings of love and anger toward that same person; interchanging optimism and pessimism about life; rebelliousness linked with submission; and idealism interspersed with cynicism.

As they learn about interpersonal relationships and socialization, most teenagers, particularly young ones, show a mixture of egocentrism, changeable self-awareness, intense dependency and pseudo-independency and pseudo-mature sexual and social roles. Frequently, many may develop crushes on coaches, teachers, counselors and others.

As they search for establishment of personal identity, maturity in social and sexual roles, emancipation from parents, occupational choices, and financial and other independence, many older adolescents may act out their frustration with hostility towards their perceived position in society and especially towards their parents. For a short time, some may turn to nicotine, alcohol, and other addictive drugs, or indulge in other escapist behavior. If they lack familial and social support, and/or have impaired personal judgment and responsibility, they may withdraw into a social isolation, pushing aside interpersonal relationships. This ultimately can result in confusion, depression, anxiety and other behavioral problems. Such at-risk teenagers may deviate into self-abusive substance misuse or sexual promiscuity, join cultist groups, take part in illegal activities, or enter diverse cults or antisocial gangs.

Sociocultural Characteristics

The powerful influence of teenage peer groups and the mass media continues to weaken the traditions and influence by parents, religion, and school on teenagers. Moreover, increasingly rapid communications such as the telephone, fax, television, and Internet facilitate the increasing spread worldwide of certain beliefs, attitudes, and practices in adolescents. Developing societies, especially, look to more powerful societies, as can be seen in the spread of North American teenage fads to Latin American youth. Anyone informed about life-styles in other countries knows that American trends about hair styles, clothing, music, fast foods, slimness, sex appeal, sexual openness, and slang are ubiquitous among many adolescents around the world.

Spiritual Characteristics

Spiritual beliefs also influence young people. Many do not easily share their beliefs and doubts with their parents, other relatives, or friends. When they do, they often justify their feelings with idealistic and moralistic values. In their search for existential significance, they constantly ask why they exist, how "close" and how "connected" they should be with others, what they should expect from themselves and others, whom they should emulate, and what might be their ultimate destiny. As they struggle in understanding the meaning of their existence, they often express masked or even overtly blunt criticism of the contradictory messages they hear from parents and other adults, especially educators, politicians, governmental officials, and religious leaders.

Stressful beliefs and aspirations about the meaning of personal existence may range from excessive ethnic and cultural and religious concerns through actual obsessions and compulsions and fears about faith. In the extreme, deviant existential and spiritual beliefs can also include individual and group practices of magical, mystic or cultist activities that may signal a need for professional help.

As some adolescents struggle while they are searching for meaningful personal identity, religious commitment, and spiritual tranquility, they may experience uncertainty, exacerbated by fear of divine punishment, which they may express with doubts, guilt, depression, or even panic. A combination of psychotherapeutic and religious counseling usually reassures and calms them.

Behavioral Patterns

The great diversity of cherished individual and group beliefs and customs reflects the numerous and contrasting scientific versus philosophical, religious, and folk systems and subsystems of health, particularly those of behavioral health. As a result, behaviors considered "normal" in one ethno-cultural group may be considered "abnormal" in another. Nevertheless, because of the increase in immigration, intercultural communications and inter-ethnic mixing, diverse ethni-cultural beliefs and practices are changing traditions within societies. For example, whereas some American-born cultist organizations (such as the People's Temple and The Native American Church) are active in Spanish-speaking countries, Hispanic folk-religious healings (such as the Mexican *curanderismo,* Cuban *santeria,* and Puerto Rican *espiritualismo)* are practiced in the midst of the sophisticated scientific and technological health care system of the United States.

Personality refers to the unique behavioral patterns of each individual, especially interpersonal and social interactions. Personality is made up of an interactive combination of heredity (chromosomes and genes,) and familial and other interpersonal relationships, as well as sociocultural, and environmental factors. Therefore, competent medical and psychiatric help is recommended to find the basis for a child's or an adolescent's unusual or self-destructive or socially deviant behavior.

End of Adolescence

An individual is considered to have ended adolescence when he or she relatively adapts to the socially determined tasks of early adulthood.

Addictive Drugs

Hypnotics/Sedatives

Names, Characteristics, and Indications: *Barbiturates (i.e., nembutal, seconal, amytal) are used in the treatment of insomnia, epilepsy, and other seizure disorders.*

Street Names: *barbiturates are called "nembies," "yellow jackets," "downers," "rainbows," "reds and blues," "devils," "tooies," "double trouble."*

Adverse Effects and Overdose/Withdrawal: *Do not produce a "high," but rather dullness, drowsiness and depression; injected intravenously they precipitate violent and delinquent behavior, may cause confusion, disorientation, skin and gastrointestinal, renal and cardiac disorders, hallucinations, uncoordinated gait, addiction. Prolonged use causes birth defects including still births in children of addicted adolescents when barbiturates are mixed with alcohol. Sudden abstinence after a prolonged use cause seizures, fever, and delirium; and overdose produces slurred speech, unsteady gait, uncoordination, impaired attention and memory. It also causes decreased blood pressure, decreased breathing and coma, all requiring urgent medical intervention.*

Tranquilizers

Names, Characteristics, and Indications: *Also called Anxiolitics, these drugs control anxiety, but do not eliminate the life stresses causing it; control muscular tensions, insomnia, convulsions, alcohol withdrawal; and increase the effects of anesthesia. Some patented names of the tranquilizers called benzodiazepines are: Valium, Librium, Klonopin, Serax, Ativan, Xanax, Dalmane, and Restoril. Other anxiolytics are carbamates (i.e., Eqvanil) and antihistaminics (i.e. Atarax, Vistaril).*

Street Names: *"Blues," "Mexican orange," and "yellows."*

Adverse Effects and Overdose/Withdrawal: *Heavy and prolonged use, particularly of benzodiazepines, may cause physical and psychological dependency, uncoordination, drowsiness, blurred vision, and decreased reflexes that produce accidents in driving and in operating machines, school underachievement, conflictual relationships, poor performance in sports and other social activities, addiction, embryonic and fetal defects. Sudden suspension of tranquilizers after a prolonged period of heavy use cause disorientation, impaired visual and auditory hallucinations, agitation and death. Misuse of tranquilizers requires professional treatment. Their mixture with alcohol cause serious illness, requires hospitalization and may be lethal.*

Opiates

Names, Characteristics, and Indications: *In the U.S., opiates or narcotics are legally prohibited even for medical prescription. Nevertheless, opiate addiction, of which 90 percent is heroin, strikes over half a million persons, particularly young adults, who usually began to use addicting drugs in adolescence or earlier. Morphine and its derivatives such as Darvon, codeine, Dilaudid, and Demerol --prescribed to alleviate pain and to promote relaxation and rest. Paregoric elixir and cough syrups have morphine derivatives and are available in many homes. Opium, as brown chunks or powder, may be smoked. Heroin, as white or brownish powder diluted in water, is injected. Other forms of opiates include tablets, capsules, solutions, syrups, and suppositories.*

Street Names: *"China white," "junk," "tar," " t," "h," "smack," "stuff, ... footballs." Users are called "hype."*
Adverse Effects and Overdose/Withdrawal: *Narcotics cause an initial euphoric "rush" followed by social isolation, decreased appetite, dry mouth, dreamlike, ecstatic, and erotic states, itching, coldness, flushing, pinpoint pupils, nasal congestion, slurred speech, impaired memory, disorientation, drowsiness, rapid pulse, slow breathing, decreased sexual drive, complicated labor, possible death of the fetus and the mother,*

depressive, psychotic, suicidal and homicidal behaviors, hypotension, coma, and death. The use of infected needles for injection of these narcotics spreads AIDS and other lethal infections. Symptoms of withdrawal appear four to six hours after suspension of heavy use of morphine and heroin and include: decreased appetite and sleep, anxiety, craving for narcotics, yawning, sweating, fever, chills, cold and hot flashes, "goose flesh" skin, tremors, muscle twitching and aching, increased respiration, lacrimation, dilated pupils, runny nose, nausea, vomiting, diarrhea, abdominal cramps, agitation, hostility, and suicidal and homicidal acts. Opiate withdrawal requires urgent medical and counseling therapies.

<u>Cocaine</u>

Names, Characteristics, and Indications: *Cocaine is a stimulant drug. In the U.S., more than 20 million persons have tried cocaine and more than eight million are currently useers. It is extracted from the coca shrub. Since prehistoric times, the leaves of this plant have been chewed to relieve fatigue and to experience euphoria. Cocaine is inhaled (snortlng), injected subcutaneously or intravenously, and smoked in cigarettes or pipes.*

Street Names: *"Coke," "nose," "candy," "girl," "The Lady," "she," "snow," "crack."*

Adverse Effects and Overdose/Withdrawal: *"Crack" pellets or powders when injected produce an intense sense of elation, and illusory elevated self-esteem and energy; though these may last only an hour, the drug can become addictive after a single trial. If inhaled or smoked, it damages the nose, sinuses, trachea and lungs, and if injected, the liver, kidneys and heart, with lethal results. Children of addicted mothers are often stillborn or born with serious birth defects. Cocaine intoxication includes euphoria, grandiosity, flushing, agitation, fever, dilated pupils, cardiac fibrillation, reactive anxiety and depression, toxic psychosis, miniaturizing objects, feeling "bugs" crawling under the skin, exaggerated sexual hunger, and suicidal and homicidal behaviors. Sudden suspension after its prolonged use* *causes fatigue, dysphoria, insomnia, restless sleep, agitation, and craving for cocaine. Such withdrawal requires urgent medical and counseling therapies.*

Hallucinogens

Names, Characteristics, and Indications: *Hallucinogens are called "psychedelics" because it is believed that they "expand consciousness" with dreamlike status and feelings ranging from euphoria to despair. These substances cause visual and auditory misperceptions (hallucinations) and derived delusions. Hallucinogens come from either natural psilocybin found in mushrooms, mescaline, peyote cactus or are derived synthetically: lysergic acid diethylamide (LSD), dipropyltryptamine (DPT), and phencyclidine (PCP). LSD has been used for experimental purposes in the treatment of severe and resistant neuroses, alcohol and narcotic addictions, infantile autism, psychopathic personalities, and to alleviate suffering of terminally ill patients with cancer.*

Street Names: *LSD is called "acid" and "blotter." PCP is called "angel dust," "peace," "peace pill,' "peace week," "super week,' "krystal," "super grass," "hog," "rocket fuel," and "TIC" or "TAC." "Ozoneal" or "tripped," is slang for the unreality caused by hallucinogens.*

Adverse Effects and Overdose/Withdrawal: *<u>Mescaline,</u> derived from the dried "buttons" or heads of the peyote cactus, can be eaten or dissolved to be used as a tea. Its synthetic form is a crystalline white powder. It produces "highs" or "trips" characterized by "expanded" perceptions, euphoria, a dreamlike state sometimes with visual, auditory, and tactile hallucinations or synesthesia ("seeing" music, "hearing" colors), fever, hypotension, depressed respiratory and cardiac activity, and vomiting. <u>Lysergic Acid Diethylamide (LSD)</u> is found in the seeds of the morning glory plant. It is sold in sugar pills, gelatin squares or on blotter paper. It causes auditory, tactile and visual hallucinations, distorted figures and geometric designs, intense and changeable opposite feelings (e.g. love and hate), exaggerated concern with religious and philosophical* *issues, depersonalization, ecstasy, and birth defects when used by pregnant women. LSD causes "bad trips," characterized by acute panic and impaired reality testing, and at times, ongoing toxic psychosis or hallucinogenic flashbacks, hallucinations, "expanded" perception of time and space, impaired sensations (paresthesia). The flashback phenomena may repeat for years after the use of the hallucinogens is discontinued, is very distressing and may lead to suicide or homicide. Phencyclidine [PCP) is another illegal hallucinogen that can be easily and cheaply assembled and sold. Small doses of PCP produce brief tranquility and euphoria, inappropriate laughter, disconnected conversation due to amnesia, apprehension and confusion or disturbed speech, uncoordinated gait, rapid heart beats, visual disturbances and exaggerated reflexes. Moderate dosages induce hypersensitivity to sound, euphoria, analgesia, nausea, floating and sensations of heat, violence, distorted body image, disturbed time and space perceptions, and loss of memory (amnesia). Higher doses cause isolation, depersonalization, illusions and hallucinations, false beliefs of persecution and grandiosity (paranoid delusions), suicidal and homicidal behaviors, facial grimaces, drooling, vomiting, hypertension, seizures, convulsions, comas with "open eyes," and even death. PCP is present in blood and urine up to a week after the last dose. Suspension of hallucinogens after prolonged use cause a distressing reexperience of impaired perceptions called flashbacks. This and toxic symptoms require medical and counselling therapies.*

Volatile Solvents

Names, Characteristics, and Indications: *Benzene, toluene, acetone and halogenated hydrocarbons are liquids used in cosmetics and in various industrial processes; they can be inhaled, tasted, or swallowed. Volatile solvents include gasoline, glue, paint thinners, varnish, nail polish removers, lighter and cleaning fluids, paint and hair sprays, cookware coating substances, and anestetic gases. They are cheap, legal and easily available, even to children. Children and adolescents are* *the most common misusers of volatile solvents. They may inhale them from a can, plastic bag, tube, or a rag held over the nose.*

Street Names: *"Poppers," "laughing gas," and "whippets."*

Adverse Effects and Overdose/Withdrawal: *Inhalants are rapidly absorbed through the lungs and affect the brain quickly. "Poppers,, which are inhaled to enhance sexual experiences, cause a feeling of hilarity, flushing, rapid heart rate, dizziness, postural hypertension, often with a loss of consciousness. Initially, the youngster may feel uninhibited, euphoric, and excited, but, later, may experience toxic symptoms. Overdoses cause dizziness, ataxia, increased self power, violence, slurred speech, floating sensation, amnesia, depression, isolation, anorexia, nystagmus, diplopia, depressed reflexes, stupor, coma, and at times death. Volatile solvents cannot be detected in the urine. Withdrawal is unknown.*

Marijuana

Names, Characteristics, and Indications: *Marijuana controls vomiting caused by anticancer drugs, and though illegal for general use, is prescribed to decrease intraocular pressure, and to control convulsions. Marijuana and hashish are illegally manufactured from the Indian plant hemp, cannabis satira. In the Far East, the plant is used in foodstuffs and beverages. Elsewhere, the cut and dried flowering tops and leaves are smoked. Marijuana's active drug is delta-9-tetrahydrocannabinol(THC) which induces euphoria. In the U.S., about one-third of the population has tried marijuana.* **Street Names:** *"grass," "pot," "hashish," "Mary Jane," "weed," "tea weed," "Kiff herb," "Ganja." "Happy or Joy sticks" are slang for marijuana sprinkled with P.C.P. and rolled into a cigarette. Youngsters who smoke cigarettes may use marijuana which can become a preliminary gateway to their self-abuse with cocaine, opiates, and other addictive and illegal drugs. Marijuana or cannabis can be eaten, smoked in "joints" (hand-rolled cigarettes), or in a pipe. The effects of cigarette inhalation appear after 20 to 30 minutes and last about three* *hours, and those of hashish begin between 30 to 60 minutes after ingestion and disappear after five to seven hours.*

Adverse Effects and Overdose/Withdrawal: *Small doses produce brief tranquility and euphoria ,frequently followed by laughter caused by inability to do planned action and subsequent disconnected conversation due to amnesia, apprehension, and confusion. Acute symptoms include increased appetite,* dry *mouth, increased pulse rate, redness of the eyes, and lowered body temperature, heightened perception of music and color, with sensations that "too many things are happening" and that time seems to "slow down," increasing awareness of self-intoxication, anxiety, confusion, laughing episodes, paranoid beliefs, depersonalization, de-realization. Its chronic use causes apathy, weight gain, impaired menstruation, decreased testosterone, bronchitis, constant coughing and lung problems, including cancer. As compared to tobacco, marijuana smoking has more carcinogens and higher potency to decrease the capacity of, the lungs to exchange gas. Cannabis can also cause "flashback," a spontaneous repetition of its adverse effects after its use is discontinued. Acute toxicity requires hospital treatment. Chronic use of marijuana may cause an amotivational syndrome characterized by apathy, and an unwillingness to finish school and other tasks. Addiction to marijuana and withdrawal after suspension of its prolonged use remain controversial. However, marijuana causes psychological dependency in many users.*

<u>Amphetamines</u>

Names, Characteristics, and Indications: *Dexedrine and benzedrine are stimulants that cause physiological and psychological dependency.*

Street Names: *"speed," "brown and clear," "pink hearts," "black beauties."*

Adverse Effects and Overdose/Withdrawal: *The oral or injected misuse of amphetamines may cause increased alertness, headaches, insomnia, poor appetite, drowsiness, agitation, grandiosity, anxiety, and panic states, false beliefs of* *persecution and omnipotence, auditory and visual hallucinations, suicidal and homicidal ideation or acts. Impaired memory and false perceptions may last for months after the drug has been discontinued and may be frightening. Abstinence after prolonged use causes fatique, dysphoria, insomnia, restless sleep, agitation, and a craving for amphetamines. Amphetamines are extrememly addicting and dangerous.*

<u>Caffeine</u>

Caffeine is present not only in coffee and tea, but also in cola drinks, chocolate, and over-the-counter (OTC) cold remedies, all easily available to youngsters. Because of their stimulant effects on the nervous system, the prolonged use of caffeine produces excessive alertness, irritability, verbal and motor hyperactivity, and an increased tolerance and addiction.

Caffeine intoxication may occur even with a daily small dose of 250 mg. of caffeine (an average size cup of coffee has 100 to 150 mg. and stimulants usually contain 100 mg per pill), but the effects of caffeine vary among individuals. Tolerance and the need for higher amounts of caffeine develop. Intoxication is manifested by restlessness, flushed face, and rapid heart beat. In excess of one gram of caffeine per day may cause insomnia, rambling speech, uncoordinated thoughts, hyperactivity, agitation, ringing or buzzing sounds in the ears, flashes of light, muscle twitching, nausea, and increased urination. The after effects of cumulative toxic doses, for example of high-caffeine content medications, can cause low blood pressure, gastritis, peptic ulcer, vomiting of blood, apprehension, and irregular pulse. Even higher doses may cause convulsions, respiratory failure and death. Caffeine intoxication is frequently misdiagnosed and mistreated as generalized anxiety disorder.

Sudden discontinuance of prolonged caffeine intake may cause throbbing headache, irritability, lethargy, and inability to experience pleasure, anxiety, and depression. These adverse effects may last four to five days.

<u>**Nicotine**</u>

Nicotine is a poisonous colorless alkaloid that is found in tobacco leaves. The U.S. Surgeon General has confirmed that nicotine in tobacco is as addictive as heroin and morphine. Self-abuse with smoking, chewing, and snuffing of tobacco unfortunately continues to increase in youngsters. The World Health Organization reports four characteristics that seem to be more common among young smokers than among non-smokers of the same age: they are more likely to have parents who smoke; they are likely to be youngsters who are not doing well in school; they are likely to have friends who smoke; and they seem to use smoking as a symbol of independence and rebellion against their parents.

Some print and electronic media have a powerful influence on smoking in adolescents and children.

Nicotine may cause a rapid addiction, sometimes coming about only after one cigarette; this is because nicotine causes physical and psychological dependency, alters mood, suppresses appetite, increases activity, and allegedly decreases stress. Cigarette smoking causes faster and greater addiction than pipe and cigar smoking, tobacco chewing, and snuffing, and is implicated in bronchitis, emphysema, cardiovascular disease, and primary lung cancer. Pipe smoking can cause cancer of the lip and tongue, and chewing and snuffing tobacco can result in oropharyngeal cancer. It is estimated that the average heavy smoker shortens his or her life by six minutes for every cigarette smoked. Tobacco smoke is dangerous even secondhand, and thus affects nonsmokers who are near smokers.

Nicotine withdrawal appears within two hours after stopping its use, may last up to several months, and is manifested by severe craving for nicotine, intense anxiety, irritability, tension, apprehension, hostility, anger, distractibility, drowsiness, insomnia, hypotension, bradycardia, hunger, and weight gain. Nicotine addiction requires medical and psychiatric therapies.

<u>**Alcohol**</u>

Although some parents refuse to recognize the fact, alcohol is a depressant, dangerous, and addicting drug. In 1990, The National Highway Traffic Safety Administration estimated that 3,361 persons aged 16 to 20 died in alcohol-related traffic accidents. The risk for alcohol dependence in youngsters is greater than for street drugs because alcohol is easily available and socially accepted.

Over 80 percent of children who drink alcoholic beverages have parents who also drink. Many parents overlook, minimize or deny that permitting their youngster to drink may initiate a dependence on alcohol and then are shocked to discover that their child has become an alcoholic.

Alcohol causes physical dependence by producing a physical and psychological need. It impairs appetite, sleep, and sexual performance. It clouds judgment and disturbs memory by depressing and eventually damaging the central nervous system. It can cause strokes, liver disease, gastrointestinal and skin ulcerations, malnutrition, and heart disease, as well as conflictual relationships with family and friends and impairment of performance at school and work.

Withdrawal appears within several hours after abstinence or decreased amounts of heavy intake of alcohol. It causes tremor, nausea, vomiting, insomnia, nightmares, illusions, hallucinations, anxiety, grand mal seizures, and agitation. It also causes delirium tremens (DT's) characterized by amnesia, disorientation, tachycardia, sweating, fever, anxiety, insomnia, vivid visual, auditory, tactile, and olfactory hallucinations, delusions, and delirium.

Self-abusive alcohol misuse and its management is discussed more fully in Chapter 11.

<u>**Management of Drug Misuse**</u>

Parents who ignore, condone, or encourage drug misuse in their children overlook the damage caused by such drugs. On the other hand, physical punishment, prolonged groundings, constant spying, deprivation of basic needs, and rejection may encourage secrecy,and increased drug self-abuse, hostility, and rebelliousness. The most effective management by parents include the following strategies:

- Identifying the physical, emotional, cognitive, and behavioral manifestations of drug misuse as listed on the preceding pages.
- Understanding the precipitating circumstances and the youngster's feelings, thoughts and motives for self-abusing drugs.
- Decreasing monetary allowances, curfew hours, phone times, parties, car use, and other privileges.
- Returning lost privileges as soon as their disciplinary effect is accomplished.
- Offering appropriate incentives and rewards to motivate drug abstinence, such as participation in music, dancing, athletics, and other activities.
- Seeking professional help if these methods fail.

Youngsters should be warned about the danger of addictive substances in a way that stresses the reality of that danger but does not exaggerate it. Children are quick to know when adults are being dishonest with them.

Finally, provide your children with interesting activities within the family, and encourage their friends to participate too. Help your children to express themselves through music, dance, sports, and other healthy activities such as scouting, but do not be surprised to find that drug usage is found even in the most closely supervised groups.

Serious juvenile addictions to alcohol and other drugs are best helped under conditions of medical supervision. Acute intoxication or withdrawal symptoms from alcohol and other drugs are nearly always provided in a hospital or certified clinic.

Narcotic Anonymous (NA) is a self-help group that follows the principles of Alcoholic Anonymous (AA) and is an important follow-up therapy for anyone giving up an addictive drug. Cocaine Anonymous (CA) is a group specifically for users of cocaine. Such groups can be effective by providing psychosocial support and education. For information for family and relatives of drug abusers, the National Institute on Drug Abuse has a hotline (phone 1-800-662-HELP) and there are support groups for these families that can be found through hospitals, clinics, and religious organizations.

Recommended Reading

American Psychiatric Association. "Diagnostic Criteria" DSM-IV, February, *1995*

Ames, L.B., IIg,F.L., and Baker, S.M., *Your Ten to Fourteen Year Old,* Dell Publishing, New York, New York,1988

Coles, R., *The Call of Stories, Teaching and the Moral Imagination,* Houghton Mifflin Company, Boston, MA.,1989

Coles, R., *Children of Crisis,* Volume I-V, Little, Brown and Company, Boston, MA, *1977*

Coles, R., *The Moral Life of Children,* Houghton Mifflin Company, Boston, MA, 1986

Coles, R., *The Political Life of Children,* Houghton Mifflin Company, Boston, MA, 1986

Coles, R., *The Spiritual Life of Children,* Houghton Mifflin, Company, Boston, *1990*

Dinkmeyer, D., and McKay, G.D., *The Parent's Handbook,* American Guidance Service, Publisher's Building, Circle Pines, MN, 1989

Dreikurs, R., *Children: The Challenge,* Penguin Books, New York, New York, 1964

Dreikurs, R., *The Challenge of Parenthood,* Penguin Books, New York, New York, 1992

Feinstein, S.C.,(ed) et.al. *Adolescent Psychiatry,* Vol 1-18, University of Chicago Press, Chicago and London, 1992

Ginott, H.G., *Between Parent and Teenager,* Avon Books, New York, New York, 1971

Harrison, M., *The Preteen's First Book About Love, Sex, and AIDS,* American Psychiatric Press, Washington, DC, 1995

Kaplan, H.I. and Sadock, B. J., *Comprehensive Textbook of Psychiatry/V,* Vol. Two, Fifth Edition, 1995

Lansdown, R., and Walker, M., *Your Child's Development from Birth through Adolescence,* Alfred A. Knopf, Inc., 1991

Leventhal, B.L., and Conroy, L. M. *Textbook of Child and Adolescent Psychiatry.* "The Parent Interview," Chapter 9 (pp. 78-84) Edited by J. Wiener, M.D., American Psychiatric Press, Washington, D.C., *1991.*

Noshpitz, J. (ed.et.al.) *The Handbook of Child Psychiatry,* Vol. 14, Basic Books, Inc., 1995

Renshaw, D. C., "Adolescent Sexuality: An Approach for All Ages," *Adolescent Medicine,* Consultant 18:11, *72-89,* November, 1978

Renshaw, D. C., *Sex Talk for a Safe Child,* American Medical Association, Chicago, Illinois, 1984

Schickedanz, J. A., Schickedanz, D.I., and Forsyth, P.D., *Toward Understanding Children,* Little, Brown and Company, Boston, MA, 1982

Uribe, V. M., and Feinstein, S. C., "Institutional Therapy for Adolescents," in Masserman, J. H. (ed): *Current Psychiatric Therapies,* Vol. 23, Grune & Stratton, Inc. 1986

Uribe, V. M., "Psychiatric Treatment of Hispanic Adolescents," *Proceedings,* Institute of Medicine of Chicago, Vol. 39, 1986

Uribe, V. M., "Short Term Dynamic Psychotherapy for Adolescents: Management of Initial Resistances," *Journal of The American Academy of Psychoanalysis,* 16 (1): 107-116, John Wiley & Sons, Inc., 1988

Uribe V. M., *Trastornos de la Personalidad en la Adolescencia, Medicina del Adolescente,* Ucros A. & Moreno C. (Editores), Colegio Mayor de Nuestra Sefiora del Rosario, Impreso por Montoya & Araujo, Bogota, 1981

Index

Bipolar disorder, 108, 110-111
Birth control devices, 79-80
Body. *See* Sexuality
Boot camp, 137
Brain. *See also* Neurotransmitters
     nervous system development and, 149-150
     sexual response and, 70
Bulimia nervosa, 22

CA. *See* Cocaine Anonymous (CA)
Caffeine, 171
Chancres, 73
Children. *See also* Adolescents; Elementary school
     age children; Infants; Toddlers
     panic attacks in, 51-52
     preschool age development of, 154-156
     separation anxiety disorder in, 39-41
     stages of development, 146-158
Chlamydia, 74-75
Choice, sexual behavior and, 72-73
Chromosomes, 146
     sexual determination by, 69-70
Chronic mercury intoxication, 110-111
Cigarettes, 85-86
     see also Addiction
Clinical psychologists, 125, 127
Cocaine, 85, 166-167
Cocaine Anonymous (CA), 174
Co-dependency, 89-90
Cognition
     in preschool age children, 155
     in primary school age children, 156-157
Cognitive concerns. *See* Emotional and cognitive concerns
Coitus. *See* Sexual dysfunctions; Sexuality
Communication
     in combating drug use, 95
     in infants, 150

Emotions, mood disorders and, 107-109
Environment, impact of, 5
Eroticism. *See* Sexuality
Estradiol, 159
Evaluation, 126
Excretion, toddlers and, 151

Family physicians, 123, 125
Family therapy, 124, 125
Fear. *See* Anxiety; Anxiety disorders; Phobic disorders;
    posttraumatic stress disorder
Females
    anorexia nervosa and, 22, 25-26
    bulimia nervosa and, 22, 26-27
    puberty in, 35
Food. *See* Eating disorders
Foreign languages, teaching of, 142
Fraternal twins, 69
Freudian psychoanalytic theory, mood disorders and, 108-109

Gangs, separation anxiety and, 40
Gender, military training and, 140-141
Gender identity, 69. *See also* Sexuality
    in preschool age children, 155
Genetics, sexuality and, 69-70
Genital herpes, 74
Genital warts, 74
Germany, adolescents as soldiers in, 139-140
Gonorrhea, 73
"Green" political parties, 140
Guilt, 6

Hallucinogens, 167-168
Healing dynamics, 132-133
Health. *See also* Diseases
    pica and, 22, 24-25
Herpes. *See* Genital herpes

and elementary school age children, 121
    and puberty, 121
Stimulant medication, for ADHD, 14
Stranger anxiety, 150
Stress
    overanxious disorder and, 41-42
    posttraumatic stress disorder and, 65-66
Substance abuse, 99. *See also* Alcohol misuse; Drug misuse
Suicide, mood disorders and, 111
Support groups, for drug misuse, 174-175
Surgeon General. *See* Novello, Antonia
Symptoms. *See* specific conditions
Syphilis, 73-74

Teenagers. *See* Adolescents
"Telegraphic style," in language development, 152-153
Temperaments, of infants, 149
Testing, by clinical psychologists, 127
Testosterone, 159
Therapists, choosing, 123-128
Therapy,
    See also Professional treatment; Treatment
    and ADHD, 14
    for blood use, 92
    for drug use, 92-93
    dynamic medical psychotherapy, 131-135
    sexual, 78-81
    termination of, 135
Toddlers
    conditions needing professional consultation, 120
    development of, 151-154
    normal anxiety in, 33-34
Toilet training, of toddlers, 151-152
Traffic accidents, alcohol related, 173
Tranquilizers, 164-165
Treatment. *See also* Professional treatment; Psychiatrists;
        therapy